THROUGH the
WINDOW of
LIFE

To Sharon –

You are loved –

Shirley
Bahlmann

6-12-2008

THROUGH *the* WINDOW *of* LIFE

SUZANNE FREEMAN
as told to Shirley Bahlmann

spring creek
BOOK COMPANY
Provo, Utah

© 2006 Suzanne Freeman & Shirley Bahlmann
All Rights Reserved.

ISBN 13: 978-1-932898-47-7
ISBN 10: 1-932898-47-6
e. 2

Published by:
Spring Creek Book Company
P.O. Box 50355
Provo, Utah 84605-0355
www.springcreekbooks.com

Cover design © Spring Creek Book Company
Cover design by Nicole Cunningham

Cover painting "New Jerusalem" by Rhett E. Murray,
courtesy of www.REMartwork.com

Printed in the United States of America
10 9 8 7 6 5 4 3 2 1
Printed on acid-free paper

Library of Congress Cataloging-in-Publication Data
Freeman, Suzanne
  Through the window of life / by Suzanne Freeman ; as told to Shirley
Bahlmann.
    p. cm.
  ISBN-13: 978-1-932898-47-7 (pbk. : alk. paper)
  ISBN-10: 1-932898-47-6 (pbk. : alk. paper)
    1.   Near-death   experiences--Religious   aspects--Christianity.   2.
Eschatology. 3.   Freeman, Suzanne (Suzanne Scholes) I. Bahlmann,
Shirley. II. Title.

BT821.3.F74 2005
248.2'9--dc22
                            2005028647

Dedication

This book is dedicated to Gary, David, Tony and Jesse. They each gave up the comforts of home and family to protect us, and also all those who have risked or gave up their lives to keep America free. To all those men and women, I say thank you.

This book is also for James, my loving husband. I appreciate all of his support in writing this book.

I thank my children, for they are my reason for living. I love them with all my heart.

Last but not least, I dedicate this book to Jesus Christ, my Savior, who loves me perfectly.

Acknowledgments

I give a big thanks to the following people for their editing and proofreading skills: Linda Pratt, Jennie Mickelson, Val Sorensen, Lannette Nielson, Jackie Brown, Larry and Gayelene Henrikson, and author Marsha Ward.

Contents

Foreword..xi

Introduction xiii

Publisher's Note..xvi

Chapter One: Too Busy To Die 1

Chapter Two: A Strange Disease 10

Chapter Three: Disaster.....................................21

Chapter Four: A Very Cold Winter....................29

Chapter Five: The Survivor................................33

Chapter Six: The Stranger 41

Chapter Seven: Invasion....................................52

Chapter Eight: Change of Address....................60

Chapter Nine: Spiritual Gifts 67

Chapter Ten: Valley of Peace 71

Chapter Eleven: Into Harm's Way 82

Chapter Twelve: Angels Among Us 88

Chapter Thirteen: Slippery Cliff 94

Chapter Fourteen: Traveling Companions 103

Chapter Fifteen: Gathering In The Flocks 110

Chapter Sixteen: Building New Jerusalem 114

Chapter Seventeen: At Christ's Side 126

Chapter Eighteen: Return to Mortality 130

About the Authors 133

Foreword

Ever since Suzanne Freeman called me "out of the blue" after reading my book *The Castaways,* we have been "pen pals." Or in today's lingo, "e-mail and phone pals." I was delighted to get to know her. Suzanne has a remarkable purity and a Nathaniel-like attribute of being "without guile." I considered myself fortunate to glean from her sweet spirit.

When Suzanne shared aspects of her intriguing near death experience, we embraced a deeper bond, like old friends reconnecting from long ago. The profundity of her message struck my heart with a familiar ring of truth. Our continuing correspondence has been rewarding, leading us over the bridge of friendship into the land of sisterhood. I am honored to write this foreword for this new book.

Those who labor to write soon learn there are choices to be made that determine the final manuscript. My visits with Suzanne verified this was true of the published account of her near-death experience entitled *Led by the Hand of Christ.* In our private communications Suzanne elaborated on insights and teachings touched on briefly or not at all in her first book. I am delighted she has decided to share more of what she learned while her spirit was "on the other side."

In this story you will see possibilities of how world events leading up to the second coming of Christ could unfold. So come, join Suzanne, her family and others as they struggle to survive a desolating sickness, marauding bands and invading armies.

Learn the necessity and "how to" of following the Spirit. Realize the miraculous power of sharing food and other resources. See the consequences of living by obedience and faith as compared to the lukewarm, the unbelieving and the antagonistic. Experience the hardships of trekking on foot, travel across mountains and plains to the site of the New Jerusalem. Witness divine protection with the returning Lost Tribes of Israel and the City of Enoch. Rejoice in reuniting with loved ones in anticipation of the return of the Messiah! Experience the love of our Savior for each of us.

Perhaps as never before you will understand the imperative of temporal and spiritual preparedness. May this work inspire you as it did me to prepare necessities in your pantry, spiritual oil in your lamps, and above all, faith in our Lord Jesus Christ.

This book will change lives! It did mine.

Sarah Hinze

Author of *Coming from the Light*
Co-author of *The Castaways* and *Songs of the Morningstars*

Introduction

Whenever most people think of the last days, they conjure up images of danger and destruction. This is to be expected, since prophecies from the beginning of time include earthquakes, floods, and other disasters. Yet when you stop to consider that life is full of exact opposites, you can find hope. As soon as someone is born, they must expect to die.

To recognize happiness, we must know what it is to feel sorrow. It wouldn't be possible to know that what we were feeling was happiness unless we had an opposite feeling to compare it to.

The bottom line is that danger will be present during the Last Days, and people will die. It is a sad fact of the last days. But in spite of all the death and destruction, there are people who are and will continue to live their lives in a way that the Spirit can guide them into safe paths. They will then be able to witness the Second Coming of the Lord.

You can stake your life on this principle, since the Lord has led many of His people out of danger. When we live the way He taught, give of ourselves and are not selfish, we will be safe from harm. We can take a lesson from the widow's mite. (Mark 12:41-44) She gave all she had, yet she didn't fear, knowing that she would be blessed for it.

These last days are a time for celebration, not a time for fear. The Lord is coming! What a wonderful time it is! Let's not fear! As you read this book, you will learn that fear is not of the Lord. Fear can actually cause greater harm if you succumb to it.

My hope is that this book will give you insight about what I was shown through the Window of Life. Have no fear, have joy, for the most loving and kind man that has ever graced the face of the earth will come back so we can live with Him forever. I am so looking forward to it. It will be a wonderful life. It is my fondest dream to have the honor of walking and talking with Him on a daily basis, to see the nail prints that were driven into his hands and feet, to feel them and to know that truly He is the Son of God. I could never tire of hearing Him laugh, to hear His perfect voice in song. Those would be highlights of my day. To be taught by the most perfect man would be something I will do anything for.

Yes we may suffer, we might go hungry, we might even die. He suffered for all my sins, and this is a small price for me to pay. If we die in His service, we will get to see Him sooner. We are blessed when we lose our lives for Him. We would have the opportunity to watch from the other side, and then be resurrected when He comes. Would you go through anything in order to see the Savior? I would be willing to go hungry for a time or have no home, knowing that my trials will eventually lead me to be in the company of the Lord. I would give up all my worldly possessions knowing that I could walk and talk with Him again. When the Lord comes we should have no fear. It will be the most exciting time in the history of the world.

I will do all I can to live my life in a way that I can be worthy of this privilege that all mankind has been waiting for, ever since Adam and Eve. Let us all spiritually prepare for His coming and not be afraid.

With this book I want to bring hope where there has been so much fear. We are in the best of times, because we will actually have the opportunity to see the Savior in all his Glory. Now is the time to prepare spiritually for his coming. Have no fear! This is the best time to be alive. With all my heart I hope that this book will bring peace to all who read it.

With all my love,
Suzanne Freeman

Publisher's Note

The information in this book was reported by Suzanne Freeman as what she experienced when she died in 1999. Some generalized events have been condensed into one representative example for clarity, and some of the names have been changed for privacy or in instances when she didn't know a specific name.

While her interview included accounts of her consciousness moving back and forth between living through the events leading to the Second Coming of Christ and watching the action unfold through the Window of Life, her story is written as though she experienced all of it.

This format provides continuity for the reader, yet is still a comprehensive record of what she saw and heard. Some lessons that Suzanne learned while watching events through the Window are italicized so readers can differentiate them from the experiences that she personally experienced.

CHAPTER ONE

Too Busy To Die

Dying is easy. Coming back to life is the hard part.

In 1999, I suffered an ectopic pregnancy and died on a hospital surgery table.

My pregnancy had gone horribly wrong from the moment the embryo attached itself to the inside of my fallopian tube. There wasn't enough room there for a baby to grow, so the tube ruptured and bled, causing me to swell up and take on the proportions of a full term pregnancy in just one day. If it wasn't bad enough that I was too big to tie my own shoes, I also had excruciating pain. To put it in basic terms, my body had turned into one big bruise. Another agonizing element of my condition was that blood enzymes, which travel harmlessly through blood vessels, were irritating my internal organs, triggering a violent reaction from my immune system to fight the "enemy." I could feel every single thrust and parry from the hostile elements battling in my body.

1

A medical team rushed me to the surgery room in an effort to save my life, but it was too late. Before they hooked me up to any monitors or gave me anesthesia, I died. My spirit floated up against the ceiling. It's a very odd sensation to gaze down at your own body, especially when it's lying on a surgery table, bloated all out of proportion.

I knew that I was dead. I also knew I couldn't stay that way. In spite of the blessed relief from the terrible burning pain of blood filling up my body in places it wasn't meant to be, my spiritual heart was aching. There were seven children at home who needed me.

My husband, a trucker at the time, would never be able to care for all of our children and provide a living for them, too. I worried that my children would have to be split up. I couldn't stand the thought of them being sent to different homes, maybe to never see each other again.

So I did the only sensible thing I could think of. I headed back toward my body. No one in the surgery room seemed to notice that I was gone yet, so I figured I could slip back inside with no one the wiser.

But someone above me knew more than I did.

Being so concerned with what I had left behind, I hadn't even thought to glance upward. My single goal was my body lying beneath me, but before I could reach it, I was stopped by a hand encircling my arm.

Startled, I looked down at the hand. It was a man's

hand, large and strong, but the most striking thing about it was the puncture wound centered in the back. Before I even raised my eyes to look at the person it belonged to, I knew that I was staring at the hand of Jesus Christ.

Filled with a sudden sense of awe, I looked up to see His blue eyes fixed on me, an expression of delight mixed with intense love emanating from their depths.

Although my heart quickened in the presence of my Savior, I tore my gaze away from Him, an unreasoning sense of panic seizing my heart. If Christ had come to get me personally, then my number must surely be up. I still didn't want to go. I couldn't. My children needed me.

I tried to pull away, struggling to break Christ's hold on my arm, anxious to get back to my body before the love and peace I felt from Him overwhelmed me and changed my mind. Because I had not been nurtured as a child, I just couldn't bear to leave my children motherless.

Christ put his other hand around my waist to restrain me. With all the love in the world poured into a few simple words, He said, "There are people who want to see you."

"Then you'll have to bring them here, because I'm not going," I said.

I didn't dare glance up at His face again for fear I wouldn't be able to stick to my resolve.

After a moment of silence, a hearty laugh rang out, startling me from my single-minded purpose. Christ was laughing! His laughter was like blending light with love, creating a sound of musical delight. His laughter was also filled with a sense of infinite reassurance that instantly calmed my fears and stopped me from trying to reach my wounded mortal shell.

"I promise I'll bring you back," Christ said, with remnants of His wonderful laughter threaded through His words.

I believed Him.

When I looked up at Him again, I was surrounded by love so complete that it was like nothing I'd ever felt anywhere on earth. Of course I would go with Him. I would follow Him anywhere.

I walked beside Christ up a flight of pure white stairs, through a pair of massive golden gates, and into a waiting crowd of my loved ones who had already passed away. There were family members I'd known on earth and others that I hadn't met there, but I recognized them anyway. There was a kind of family connection that resonated in my soul.

We all shared hugs and exclamations of delight at being reunited. Once I'd had a chance to greet everyone, Christ showed me more of this beautiful realm I was in, and my family followed along behind us.

I toured various heavenly cities, and Christ acted as the perfect host while introducing me to several people who had been prominent in earth's history, including the prophet Enoch, Joseph of Egypt, and the founding fathers of the United States of America.

Then Christ led me into a white room, so white that I'm sure it would have hurt my eyes if I'd been in my physical body. It was brighter than the sun beating down on snow at mid-day. It was so entirely white that it was difficult to tell where the wall ended and the floor began. Every surface in the room was of equal brightness, all clean, shining, and glowing white.

Then Christ gestured toward a large screen at one end of the room. Even though the screen was framed by what appeared to be ornate woodwork, the screen's uniform whiteness nearly blended with everything else in the room.

The screen would have been easy to overlook, but once Christ pointed it out to me, it was all I could see. Although there was nothing inherently dangerous about it, I got a cold shiver as I measured its height and breadth with my gaze. It was at least four feet by eight feet. It seemed as though the screen stared back at me with its cold white eye.

I turned to Christ, instinctively putting my back toward the ominous screen. Somehow I knew that it was not there for my peace and comfort.

Christ's eyes softened as he gazed on my apprehensive face. He knew just what I was thinking. He always knows what we're thinking.

"Suzanne," he said in a voice that caressed my name with infinite tenderness. He pointed at the screen. "Through the Window of Life, I can show you some scenes from the Last Days of the world, things that may happen before I come again."

My heart constricted as I cried out, "I don't want to know!"

I have never been one of those people who are overly interested in what is to come in the future. In high school, I'd read the novel *Fahrenheit 451* by Ray Bradbury. I found it disturbing to read of a future portrayed as a place so bleak and heartless that I was in no hurry to get there.

As for the advent of Christ's Second Coming, I had only read what was in the scriptures. None of the events leading up to his actual appearance sounded very good.

My nerves tight, because I feared His answer, I looked up at the gentle face of Christ. "Do I have to see it?"

Christ pulled me into an embrace that melted every one of my concerns with His loving reassurance. "Of course not."

I breathed a sigh of relief, basking in the unconditional love that surrounded me like a soft, warm quilt. Christ pulled a few inches away and smiled down at me, His eyes gentle and wise. "But you will save a lot of lives if you do."

The quilt suddenly felt tight, nearly suffocating, and I turned away, instinctively trying to draw in air, even though my spirit didn't need to worry about breathing. I was so new to being dead that I reacted as if I were still in my physical body.

The white screen caught my eye. As I stared at it, it seemed to grow bigger, to loom higher and higher until I felt that it would swallow me whole.

Alarmed, I took a step back and nearly lost my balance. Christ took hold of my arm, His gentle touch warm and reassuring. I glanced down at His hand and again noticed the wound in the back of it, the tortuous wound that had held him up on the cross for hours, his body pulling down against the cruel metal spike that wouldn't let go. He had suffered for me, and now I was cringing at a simple thing He'd asked me to do.

I straightened and turned toward my Savior with a sudden calm resolve. With Christ at my side, I wouldn't be afraid. "Yes, I'll do it."

Christ smiled, a perfect radiant smile that beamed light, brightening the room even more.

"Will You stay with me?" I asked.

Christ encircled me with His arm as we turned to face the screen. "I'll be with you all the way," He said.

As we watched, side by side, the screen shaded to a pale hue, a light blue that gradually grew in intensity until it became the bright blue of a mid-summer sky. Bits of marshmallow white smudged the edges of the screen, moving inward and converging until they formed clouds that drifted toward me, as stout as sailing ships, as unsubstantial as sea foam. They surrounded me, shifting shape and brushing up against me, sending prickles up and down my arms. The clouds swirled and parted, closed, opened again, changing my focus until I felt myself flying through the air among them. I was falling.

This wasn't what I had expected. But Christ had never said that I'd be sitting in a padded theater seat with a bucket of popcorn and a soda. I thought I'd be watching a movie like in a movie theater, but now it was clear I would see the things Christ wanted to show me in a more personal way than I had first imagined. Yet, as I fell, I realized that I was unafraid. I could no longer see Christ, but I could feel Him beside me, as He promised He'd be.

The clouds moved constantly, swirling against my face, then gliding away in a slow ballroom dance. They shifted and parted beneath my feet until I could see the world spread out below, the oceans and continents bright blue and green, alternately shadowed by clouds, then bathed in bright sunlight.

As I flew downward, the world stretched ever farther, from horizon to horizon, until the curve of the earth's surface was lost in the distance. Mountains rose, and rivers sparkled in the sunlight. A small town came into focus.

As I drew closer, I recognized my hometown of Pleasant View. When I was closer still, I saw that I was headed straight for the roof of my own house. Instinctively, I crossed my arms in front of my face and braced for impact.

CHAPTER TWO

A Strange Disease

The next thing I knew, I was headed out the door of my house with a pot of soup carried with a hot pad in each hand to hold onto the handles. Blended with the aroma of savory soup was the scent of crusty sourdough bread wafting out from a piece of rewashed tin foil I'd wrapped around a fresh loaf and balanced on top of the lid.

When I reached the street, I turned left and kept walking, heading for the Muncie home. Several people in their family were sick, including their mother, Marie.

As I made my way down the street, mud clung to the bottom of my feet, each step adding another layer of brown clay to the soles of my shoes, building up to an ever-increasing thickness until its own weight made it drop off. It would have been more convenient to drive my car, but I hadn't driven for so long that the thought barely crossed my mind. There was almost no gasoline to be had. If you could manage to find any, it was terribly expensive. So cars sat idle in driveways and abandoned along the streets, staring with dull, unseeing headlights as people walked or rode bicycles from place to place.

When I finally reached the Muncie home, my arms were sagging with fatigue from carrying the heavy soup. I was afraid if I set it down, I might not be able to pick it up again, so I tapped on their door with the toe of my soggy shoe. _Thud, thud, thud._

The door opened a few hesitant inches. Through the crack I could see a thin teenage girl in jeans so baggy she had to cinch them in with a belt. I gave her a warm smile just as a voice from the back of the house croaked, "Barbara! Don't let anyone in!"

"I've brought food," I said, holding the pot a few inches higher as though that would help Barbara see it better. The sourdough bread wobbled on top, and Barbara flung the door wide and darted her hand out to steady it. Her eyes grew large with desire as she saw the crust of bread peeking out from the edge of the foil. "There's food, Mom!" Barbara called back over her shoulder.

Uneven footsteps sounded from somewhere down the hall. Harsh hacks from a throat scraped sore from coughing punctuated the footfalls. A painfully thin woman tottered into the room. Her eyes jumped from the pot to my face and back again, with longing and caution battling in her eyes. Marie was so thin that I hardly recognized her. We hadn't been to church together in at least a year, ever since public gatherings were banned when the strange illness that gripped our town was declared to be an epidemic.

"You aren't sick, are you?" Marie asked.

"No, and neither is my family," I assured her. "This is good food."

Marie reached out and took the pot from me at the same moment Barbara pulled the bread in close to her chest. Marie turned and stumbled toward her kitchen.

"I can carry that for you," I offered, moving a step closer.

"No!" Marie's voice was harsh. "Sorry. This is just fine. We'll have your pot out on the porch tomorrow for you to pick up."

"All right," I said, and turned to go.

"Thank you," Marie called out.

I turned back to give her a warm smile. "You're welcome."

"God bless you," she whispered.

Barbara didn't even try to stop the tears from rolling down her face as she shut the door.

On my way home, the rain started again. I hunched my shoulders and slogged through the slippery streets, raising my hand now and then to brush the water away from my eyes. I hadn't bothered to bring an umbrella with me. It wouldn't have been a bad idea, since the rainfall was nearly constant. Even though it was late summer, there were no crops growing in the fields outside of town. For months it had been too wet to plant. If anyone had gotten anything planted, the seeds would be rotting from the excess water that drenched us day after day.

There was no food in the stores, either. Not only had heavy summer rains washed out several roads, but truckers refused to drive into places gripped by this strange new disease that had no cure.

Farm animals suffered from the deluge, too. They were often caught in bogs of mud so thick and unforgiving that they couldn't get themselves out. Either they wore themselves to exhaustion in their efforts to escape, finally surrendering their weary muzzles to the deep oblivion of the suffocating mud, or else they broke bones or ruptured organs in their desperate attempt to break away from the grip of waterlogged fields and paddocks. Those that didn't die from being caught in the mud were just as likely to starve to death.

I hurried inside the back door of my house, giving my hair a brisk shake to get rid of water droplets that dripped down my neck in cold rivulets. My husband, James, met me with a towel. I accepted it with gratitude and rubbed my head as dry as I could. Then I draped the towel over my shoulders and headed for the bedroom to change into something dry.

"Mike Fiddler died today," James said.

I stopped and rubbed a weary hand against my forehead. "That makes five this week."

James nodded. "Reports on the radio say that only two percent of the population are dying from this outbreak."

I whirled to stare at James, my eyes wide with disbelief. "That's ridiculous! In Pleasant View alone, the death rate's around thirty percent! How could it be less anywhere else?"

James put his hands out, palms up, in his own defense. "It's just what they're saying."

In an instant, as though someone whispered the answer in my ear, I knew why the broadcast reports were wrong. It was deliberate. Those issuing the reports feared total panic if the truth was known. The level of devastation that the illness had brought upon the United States' population was unparalleled by anything except maybe the Black Plague in Europe.

I turned and headed for my room.

"Uh, Suzie, Nick Bender was here while you were out," James said.

"What did he want?" I asked.

"He wondered if you could make something for his Mom to eat, because she's so sick she can't get out of bed."

My shoulders slumped with weariness, but I knew I would do it. Nick was a skinny freckled boy about fifteen years old who had often played with my son

Joseph in better days. Nick's father had already died of the disease, and Nick was the only surviving child. I couldn't tell him no.

Instead of going to my room, I headed for the kitchen, my footsteps accompanied by the steady pounding of rain on the roof.

I didn't resent sharing our food with Nick or anyone else who needed it. I've always believed in storing food in my home, so I had enough to share. I buy cases of food on sale. Besides the security of having extra food reserves, it's cheaper to feed my large family this way, because just about everything they eat was bought at a discount.

Storing food is not a crazy new fad. Check the history books, or check the Bible. Throughout history, people relied on food stored from bountiful summer and fall months to sustain them through the winter, or even longer.

Joseph of Egypt stored food during seven years of plenty and fed a whole civilization through seven years of famine. (Genesis 41:29-57)

Just because our grocery stores are almost always stocked with more things than we want is no reason for us not to store food, clothes, and other things we may need in the future. Retail stores are convenient, but I wouldn't stake my life on them. In times of crisis, such as hurricanes or earthquakes, the grocery stores are emptied of their contents in a matter of hours.

I know many families who have fallen on hard times because of unemployment or other unforeseen circumstances that depleted their budget, but food storage saw them through. I've also heard of instances where people who survived a natural disaster and had some non-perishable food stored in their homes. They were able to feed their families and share with others until roads and electrical lines were repaired.

If we make it a habit now to always have some extra food and clothing stored away, no matter the amount, and to share what we have, then it will not be hard for us to share with others when a crisis arises.

As Marie had pointed out, another reason people relied on me to help feed them was that my family was not sick. No one I knew of was willing to accept food from homes that were afflicted with disease. I wasn't the only one sharing food, but I felt it was my duty to contribute. I was glad to be of help, and grateful that my family was well.

Neither doctors nor scientists had made any progress toward finding a cure for the strange disease that plagued the nation. No antibiotics touched the illness; there was no medicine for it at all. It was touted as a virus, but there seemed to be new strains discovered at frequent intervals.

As I reconstituted some instant mashed potatoes and opened a package of dehydrated onions, a thought struck me that was so profound in its simplicity that I stopped in the middle of measuring the soup ingredients and stared at the pan of water waiting on the stove.

Fear was the main cause of the illness that plagued the nation.

With sudden clarity, I recalled a story that my mother had told me about a man who declared that he was going to die with his boots on. Years later, he was out fishing in a boat, fell out, and drowned. Sure enough, he had his boots on.

Another lady I knew was paranoid about getting cancer. It seemed that every time she and my mother would talk about illnesses, she'd turn the subject to cancer. "I'm so afraid of getting cancer," she'd say. "I really don't want to die of cancer." Well, one day she was diagnosed with cancer and soon died from it.

Entertaining fear invites illness, accidents, and troubles that we don't have to have. Fear attracts and acts as a conductor for devastation, just as water is to electricity. Anyone in his right mind would not choose to put on a suit of armor and stand out on a hill in the rain during a thunderstorm. You'd just be asking to get struck by a bolt of lightning.

If we use fear as a conductor, we will attract all kinds of fear-based events into our lives.

If there is trust in the Lord, we will never fear. Faith can move mountains, so why wouldn't it be able to keep us well? (Matthew 17:20) We must know that Christ is on our side, that He is willing and able to save us from anything. We must have complete trust in Him, because only through Him can we be saved.

With Christ on our side, what is there to be afraid of? Whether we die, or whether we live to see the Second Coming of Christ, it won't matter, as long as we love the Lord. If we're doing what we're supposed to, there is no reason to fear at all. When we die, the stress and earthly struggle are over for us. We won't ever stop being, we just live on in another dimension, a wonderful place where there is no pain and we are surrounded by great happiness. We will be able to meet our Maker with no regrets. What a great day that will be! What a grand adventure! If we'd all just exercise faith in God, we would all be much better off.

The only reason a child of God should ever fear is if they are not doing the things they know are right, or if they're deliberately doing things they know are wrong.

Charged with energy from the insight I'd just received, I quickly finished my task of making a simple, yet nourishing, soup for Nick and his mother. I put on a hat and raincoat before I headed out into the wet world outside of my home.

When I got back from my errand, I was anxious to change into something dry and maybe lie down for a few minutes. But all thoughts of rest vanished when I saw the shape of a body underneath a blanket in my living room. Had one of my children taken sick?

When I moved around the couch to get a better look, I was startled to see my friend Stacey lying there, her face pale, the large, pregnant belly that had preceded her the last time I'd seen her now reduced to a soft hill. Her eyes closed, she cradled a tiny bundle in one arm.

"Stacey!" I cried. "When did you have your baby?"

It looked as though it took great effort for her to open her eyes. "I don't know. Maybe an hour ago." Then her eyes fell closed again.

I knew that Stacey always had her babies at the hospital. Stacey looked so pale and weak that I couldn't imagine the hospital staff sending her away in this condition.

"Why aren't you still in the hospital?" I asked, kneeling beside her.

Stacey gave me a weak smile. "You haven't been to the hospital lately, have you?" she asked. "There are sick people packed into every room and more spilling out into the halls. There's no room for people to have babies."

"Then where . . ."

"Oh, I went there to have my baby, all right. They tried to make a sterile place for me in a utility closet by the back door. As soon as Jillian was born, they said I had to leave. They were afraid that she might get the sickness if we didn't go right away."

Stacey turned her head and gazed at her infant,

still wrinkled and damp-haired from birth. When she sighed and laid her head back on the couch cushion, tears squeezed out from under her eyelids. "I just needed a place to rest, Suzie. My husband's gone to look for work, and I didn't think you'd mind."

My heart flooded with compassion. "Of course I don't mind," I said. Stacey was obviously not up to any more questions, although I was curious as all get-out as to how she got to my house. Her legs were spattered with mud, and her shoes were gone. A quick glance at the doorway showed them lying by the door in two haphazard little bundles coated with mud. Had she walked the whole way, just after giving birth?

This was no time for questions. There were more important things to deal with at the moment.

"I'll go make supper for all of us," I said. "You can stay here as long as you'd like."

Stacey didn't answer. Eyes closed, jaw slack, she breathed in that deep, steady rhythm of complete exhaustion.

CHAPTER THREE

Disaster

A few weeks later, autumn was upon us. I stood at the kitchen sink, up to my elbows in dish soap suds, when James rushed in from the other room. "Two dams just broke," he announced.

"What do you mean they broke?" I asked, hardly believing his words.

"Well, there was an earthquake first. Cracked them both right down the middle. All the water built up behind them did the rest. There's massive flooding." James was nearly breathless with the news. "Other dams are on the verge of giving way. There's just been too much rain."

I stared out the window at the sparse rust-colored leaves drooping on the tree limbs outside my kitchen. The once crisp fall colors were dulled by the rain that had poured down on us all summer long. My heart was heavy for those who had been in the path of the powerful water unleashed from the broken dams.

James hurried back to his radio, but I didn't have the heart to follow him.

My perception shifted slightly, and I suddenly felt as if my kitchen window had turned into a miniature Window Of Life. The leaves outside merged together into a deep, earth-heart red, roiling in a slow spin as though I was looking into the bowels of the earth.

Suddenly a stream of molten rock shot up from an ancient volcano, so old that its sides were carpeted with deep green vines and trees as tall as eight-story buildings. The lava hissed and spewed onto the growing plants, scorching the leaves until they smoked and shriveled, then toppling the trunks of the jungle giants into a pile of huge matchsticks. They smoldered as the lava buried them with its fiery body, working its way down the mountainside in search of new victims.

I saw more volcanoes erupting, their huge mouths open heavenward. Quiet for centuries, they now spewed red-hot lava over villages and towns.

To my amazement, I even saw mountains that had never been volcanoes explode, molten rock scarring their sides and spreading over the countryside. People ran in blind terror, abandoning their homes, screaming with pain and horror as hot lava met human flesh, while I stood in my kitchen, alone and trembling.

The unlikely movie screen of the window shifted to a city that shook as badly as my fingers trying to steady themselves on the edge of the kitchen sink. I saw a tall gray building on the city skyline crack and sway, sending people screaming from the streets beneath its menacing shadow. They stampeded in all directions. In their haste to save themselves, teenagers and adults pushed children and the aged out of their way, knocking down anyone weaker or smaller and leaving them to be trampled. I saw many lying on the ground, bleeding, broken, and helpless. Those who'd pushed them so roughly aside fled from one crumbling structure only to intersect the path of another.

Some of the wounded were able to pick themselves up and limp or crawl away, their mouths open in horror as they sought a safe place to hide.

A blue four-door sedan careened down the street, dodging bricks and rubble. As I watched, it slowed, then came to a shuddering stop beneath the cracked gray building. A young man leapt out of the car and stared up at the uneven structure. Terrified people streamed around him as the building sagged on a damaged foundation.

The young man seemed unsure of what to do next. His perplexed face made me wonder if he even knew why he'd stopped in the first place.

Another shudder rocked the ground, and the building danced in the aftermath, an eerie sway that made it look like it was made of rubber. The streets were deserted by now, populated only by the dead and an uncertain young man standing by his old blue car.

Suddenly, a woman's face appeared in one of the gray building's lopsided windows. As soon as the young man's eyes met hers, he dashed toward the building, disappearing inside the swaying structure without a moment's hesitation. After a few minutes, the woman stumbled out of the crooked doorway, a bleeding child sagging from her arms, two other children hanging onto either side of her, their faces smeared with dirt and tears. The young man followed, supporting a teenage boy who favored his left leg. It looked like it was broken.

The young man shepherded the family to his car. The mother slid into the back seat with the child still in her arms. The other children crowded in after her as the young man helped the wounded teenager into the front seat.

I suddenly knew with certainty that the young man had never met these people before, yet in her desperation, the woman accepted his help without hesitating.

The young man slipped into the driver's seat, gunned the engine, and roared away from the curb just as the crippled building broke and fell, scattering bricks and shooting window glass skittering along the street after them. Dust filled the air, a choking cloud that obscured my view.

When it cleared, I saw another earthquake in a different part of the world. It ripped the ground apart, releasing huge fountains of water that whooshed up to the heavens with a roar, then slammed back to earth and tore across the land, destroying everything in their paths.

The scene shifted to a monster tornado, its swirling cone of deadly wind tearing the sky in two as it roared toward a town crouched on a flat prairie. People with faces distorted by fear dashed into underground shelters, slamming and bolting the doors behind them. Their ears were deaf to the cries of others who pounded on the locked doors, begging to be let in, even as the savage wind tore at their clothes and pulled their hair up into a tangled mess.

Some of the victims were plucked up by the fierce wind and flung in among the whirling debris, while others staggered off across the fields until they were either caught up into the whirlwind or crushed by falling objects. The tornado swirled over the land with complete disdain for human life.

Floods, earthquakes, and tornados often occurred in places that one would never think they could happen. I saw a half dozen people running down the street of a town in a mountain valley, fleeing for their lives, a huge tornado breathing down their necks. Typically, tornados don't form in mountainous areas. The theory is that the high winds need a wide, flat place to move around in. Mountains tend to get in their way.

A car swerved to the side of the road beside the tornado's escapees. A door popped open and the driver screamed, "Get in!" The runners dove into the car and it sped down the road, doors flapping, keeping just ahead of the killing wind.

My heart rejoiced at the glimpses of those heroes willing to risk themselves to save another. They didn't consider their own fate before helping someone else, doing all they could to relieve the suffering of others.

Watching people trying to save themselves was more common than seeing people try to help others. I even saw parents abandon their children in panicked efforts to escape whatever disaster was on their heels.

Hard times will either make or break a person. In order to know who someone really is deep down inside, they must be caught by surprise. They will either be selfish or selfless. When confronted with sudden, lethal danger, will they think only of themselves, will they think of their family, or will they risk their lives to help a total stranger?

The destructive scene on my kitchen window shifted, similar to the way your eyes re-focus and see a picture of an optical illusion. It's the same picture, but now your brain processes the information a little differently.

I stared in wonder as scores of angels came into focus, angels waiting and wanting to help, but their heavenly aid was bound and useless because people weren't even thinking to pray. All it would have taken was a single uttered prayer, a "Please help us, God!" and the angels would have been right there, holding up the buildings, redirecting the lava flow, or quieting the winds.

If we do not fear, and call upon God in faith, the destruction will either pass us by, take us quickly home to Him, or at least not destroy things that may be of vital importance to those who survive.

The only way to make it through disasters is to exercise selflessness. Be more concerned about others than you are about yourself. Don't even think about dying. When you see people who need help, go to their aid. Then, whether you live or die, your heart and soul will be in the right place.

The scene shifted to one of the aftermath of a devastating tornado. Flattened houses were interspersed with animal carcasses, upended automobiles, and trees tossed into bizarre poses that made them look like alien skeletons. I noticed a few people picking their way through the rubble. They would occasionally bend and lift up a glittering item of jewelry, a radio, or a piece of twisted silver that may have once been a teapot. They'd slip their finds into pockets or packs, then proceed through the destruction, eyes searching the tangled remains of various houses to take things that weren't theirs.

I saw a lot of stealing by people who tried to justify it as saving their lives, but the things they took were not immediately life sustaining. These people exhibited no remorse or any thought of ever giving back to anyone for the things they took. All they had in their minds was self-preservation.

Many people have been taught by example or the media that they are entitled to everything they want. They pass these teachings along to their children. People generally do not want to deprive their families, so they give them things that ought to be worked for and earned on their own. The people I saw were stealing their own souls, casting them out of Heaven for eternity. The Heavens weep when they look down on actions such as this.

Most people don't generally acknowledge the hand of God in our lives, and they don't recognize what they have been blessed with, until they no longer have it. There are those who won't believe it is the Last Days until the disasters strike.

CHAPTER FOUR
A Very Cold Winter

A chill wind rattled the windows. I pulled a knitted scarf tighter over my head, trying to make it give me more warmth.

It was the coldest winter in memory, and there was no natural gas to heat our home—or anyone else's, either.

James stumbled in through the door, his breath clouding and his nose red from the bitter cold outside. His arms were full of split wood, and he shoved the door closed with his shoulder. It didn't seem to make a difference to the indoor temperature whether the door was closed or open, but at least it blocked the wind and snow from getting inside.

I hurried to the wood stove and pulled the door open. James dropped the wood on the floor, then began feeding some into the flame.

"I think you should bring in some coal," I said.

"Later tonight," James said. "While we're awake, we

can stoke the fire. We'll save the coal to maintain the fire overnight."

James was right. We should save our coal to use overnight, when the fire might go out without us noticing, but it was hard to wait. My fingers felt numb from the cold.

The reason James was even around to split wood for us was because he was out of work. So was everyone else I knew, at least for paid jobs. There were still doctors and nurses, and people who sewed, and builders, but they never got paid anymore. It didn't really matter if anyone had money anyway, since there was nothing to buy on the store shelves.

The nation's economy was in shreds. The most valuable commodity we had was our stored food. I could only imagine how awful it might be for the survivors of the natural disasters that were without homes, without food, and without clean water to drink.

Cleanup efforts were slow, and sometimes non-existent. Sadly, we often don't prepare spiritually or temporally for hard times, even though we have been warned for many years to do so. But because of the seemingly endless warnings we receive, too often we turn a deaf ear.

So far our home had been spared from the catastrophes, and I was grateful. Even though James was out of work, he had plenty to do. Not only did he keep busy splitting the wood in our stockpile to the

right size to burn, he and other able-bodied men also
hauled wood for those who didn't already have some
stored in their backyards. It was good that he was
an ambitious man, because it seemed that he could
only be outside as long as he was moving. "If I stop,"
he joked, "I might just freeze in place. Then everyone
would know I was taking a break."

"Mom?" Our youngest son poked his head out
from beneath the covers of the living room hide-a-bed.
It was folded out next to our woodstove, as close as it
could safely get. We all slept in the living room now,
with as many of us on the hide-a-bed as would fit. All
the others slept together in a nest of sleeping bags on
the floor. The nights got so cold it felt that if we didn't
share our body warmth, we might freeze to death in
our sleep.

"What do you want, Joseph?"

"Can I have some hot chocolate?" Although his
voice was deepening as his body matured, he sounded
as hopeful as a young child, his hands clasped under
his chin in supplication. A little shiver ran through his
body.

"There's not much left," I said. "How about if I make
you some warm broth for now? I've got lots of beef
stock powder."

His face fell, but he nodded.

I felt a twinge of sadness for my son, but I really felt
the beef stock would be better for him right now.

"Come out and help me chop wood for the Jensens," James said.

"But it's cold!" Joseph protested.

"Work warms you up," James said. "Come on."

"I'll get the broth ready for you to drink before you go outside," I said, moving toward the kitchen. "And we'll have some hot chocolate just before bed."

Joseph sighed, shrugged off his covers, and searched on the floor beside the couch for his shoes. If it turned out to be a long winter, I may have to end up offering my family hot water to keep them from freezing, but I knew that trusting in the Lord was the best thing to do.

The bitter cold we had to endure was actually a blessing in disguise, sent to help us prepare for what was to come. Those who had no homes, yet were doing their best to follow the teachings of Christ, were entitled to be cloaked with the warmth of God. Having faith in Him and knowing that He has the power to save, even in hard times, is a great comfort. Blessings from Heaven are available to those who ask for them.

CHAPTER FIVE
The Survivor

Spring brought relief from the crippling cold, but it also brought a fresh deluge of rain. Snowmelt from the deep winter drifts mixed with the rain, adding such an incredible burden to the reservoirs and dams that hasty repair efforts from the year before refused to hold and more of them gave way.

One late spring day, frantic pounding on my front door sent me scurrying to open it. My neighbor, Natalie, stood there, wringing her hands as she searched my face with frantic eyes. "Suzanne, we're going to Crooked Creek to get my parents," she said.

Crooked Creek was a little town on the banks of a small river by the same name. Unfortunately, it was located downstream from a dam that had given way just the day before. The flooded settlement was three hours away by car, and no one I knew had a vehicle with that much gas.

"How will you get there?" I asked.

"We've got that gas tank on the farm," Natalie said, absently gesturing behind her as though her farm were next door instead of on the outskirts of town. I remembered the fifty-gallon barrel they had suspended on a metal rack, a gas hose fastened low on one end.

"We haven't used all of it, and there's enough left to make the trip," Natalie said. Her chin quivered. "Crooked Creek's been flooded."

I nodded to let her know I'd already heard the news.

"I told Roger that we had to get my parents and bring them back here to live with us." Tears welled up in Natalie's eyes. "We haven't been able to get through to them, and I don't know what we'll find when we get there. Would you come with me?"

When I hesitated, Natalie reached out and grabbed my hand. "Please, Suzanne." Tears spilled over her cheeks, and she bit her lip before she said, "We should be back tomorrow, no matter what."

"Let me go talk to James," I said, giving Natalie's hand a squeeze.

James felt that Natalie needed me to go with her. After he agreed to maintain the home front, I climbed into Natalie's car and we headed for Crooked Creek with Roger at the wheel.

When we finally arrived, I was astonished to see that even the vision I'd seen in my kitchen window the previous autumn hadn't prepared me for the real life devastation spread before me. It was as if the stricken land had a spirit of doom hanging over it, a tangible hopelessness that made the destruction even more soul-wrenching. Houses weren't even recognizable as houses. Parts of them were scattered about, broken timber sticking out of the black mud like wooden bones. When we stepped out of the car, a vague smell of rottenness wafted past my nose. I detected occasional odors of sewage on the teasing wind, and the smell of decay.

I stared around in amazement, my stomach sick at the sight of so much ruin. An easy chair upholstered in brown slime sat in the precarious company of a car body that was upended in the thick muck like a clumsy, oversized lamp. A kitchen table surrendered, its two remaining legs sticking helplessly into the air. Evidence of people's daily lives was scattered everywhere.

Natalie started across the muddy ground toward a few people gathered in the distance who were moving one way, then the other, back and forth as if they had no real purpose. Natalie's body leaned forward in haste, but her steps were sluggish as she fought to free her feet from the sucking mud. Roger was right behind her. I followed at a slower pace.

By the time I caught up to them, they stood at the edge of the creek with some of the flood survivors. Natalie had her arm around the waist of an older man, and I assumed she'd found her father. The two of them stared into Crooked Creek, where the water had crept back between its banks, but was still brown and thick with mud and debris. A log rolled past, a limb cracking as it struck the front of a partially submerged tractor. Another log followed, this one without any stiff, outstretched limbs to scrape the banks.

One of the men reached out with a long, hooked pole. It looked as if he meant to pull the second log in to shore. I wondered why he wanted it, until all at once, my heart leapt up into my throat when I realized that the log was not a log at all, but a human body.

I stared at the group of damp and bedraggled people, their eyes red from weariness, or crying, or both. It was only then that I noticed several bodies already laid out along the shore, camouflaged with streaks of mud.

My heart swelled with compassion. I stepped down the bank and into the water so I could help guide the hook to its goal. The water gurgled around my warm body, welcoming me with an icy embrace, nearly paralyzing me with cold. I gasped and grabbed the grappling hook. It wobbled and dipped my hands into the brown creek, making them nearly numb from their brief contact with the freezing water.

I gasped again, then steadied my feet on the river bottom as I faced upriver. The body floated closer. I guided the hook toward the muddy torso, but before the hook got a good grip, the body was close enough for me to touch. I grabbed onto it and pushed it toward shore. The skin beneath the smeared fabric was as stiff as wood, and so cold it made me shiver. Several hands reached down to pull the body up and lay it beside its fellow victims.

Each body I helped retrieve seemed to weigh more than the one before. Finally, my heart heavy and my limbs weary, I glanced upstream to see if there were any more bodies. I instantly wished I hadn't, because I saw a small body no more than two feet long floating toward me.

Oh, no. Not a baby!

It wasn't rolling over and over, or looking down into the depths of the creek. It floated along on top of the water as peaceful as if it were riding in a baby buggy. The little pink face with closed eyes made it look as though the baby was merely sleeping. But no warm-blooded creature could survive in this icy water for long.

Even though I knew the little spirit was safe with God, tears burned the back of my eyes. If I hadn't been the one to spot the child, I may have let someone else pull her out, but by now she was so close to me that I could see she had no clothes on. Whether the flood waters had savagely ripped them from her body, or whether she'd been caught in the flood in the middle of a diaper change, I didn't know. I could only hope that she hadn't been alone when the water hit, adding even more fear to the trauma of drowning.

With aching heart, I reached out to pull the little body into my arms. When I touched her shoulder, I was startled to feel warm flesh.

Something wasn't right. All the other bodies had been as cold as skinned peaches right out of the refrigerator. And they'd had clothes on. Why was this little naked baby so warm?

The instant the question formed in my mind, my perception shifted, as though I now saw events from the other side of a two-way mirror. My breath caught when I focused on two angels, one on either side of the baby, holding her little body in their large, warm hands, sheltering her skin from the frigid water.

It was now my turn to take charge of the child. I took hold of her arm and pulled her little body in close to mine, an instinctive gesture of protection. The angels pulled back, their smiling faces full of love.

My eyes went past the angels, my sight reaching far beyond my immediate surroundings. I saw both guardian angels and destroying angels in various places of the world, some helping mortals, some exacting justice. The destroying angels carried big swords, and their clothes resembled the costumes I'd seen in paintings of executioners from two thousand years ago. Chills ran down my spine as I stared at the wondrous sight. At last I blinked, and the images faded away. Even the angels who'd stood in the water in front of me just a moment before were gone.

I stared down at the baby's peach-pink face in time to see her tiny eyelids flicker. Then they fluttered open and the baby stared at me with beautiful green eyes. After taking a moment to search my soul, she gave me a big smile. Although the smile was big for her, it looked just like a smaller version of the ones the angels had bestowed on me.

"She's alive!" I shouted.

There was a second of shocked silence, then a flurry of activity. Someone reached down with a sweater spread across his hands, and I surrendered the baby to the slightly damp nest, still warm from the man who'd given it up for the sake of the baby.

Then a woman screamed, "That's my baby!" She rushed forward and took the child, sweater and all, into her arms. Weeping and laughing, she held her little daughter close. Then her eyes flickered toward Heaven and she sank to her knees on the muddy riverbank. She was soon joined by all the other work-weary survivors.

With smiles of joy, and eyes full of wonder, the people by the creek lifted their faces toward Heaven and thanked God for the miracle of the living baby pulled from the killing waters.

I climbed out of the water, too numb to even feel my legs.

We soon discovered that the destroying angels had passed over Natalie's parents, but just barely. Her mother had sustained a serious gash on her leg, had many small cuts over her body, and suffered from several deep and painful bruises. On our way back to Pleasant View, Natalie's dad cradled his wounded wife in his arms.

CHAPTER SIX

The Stranger

A couple of days after returning with Natalie's parents, I pulled open the kitchen door and breathed in the heavenly scent of warm earth and greening leaves. There wasn't a trace of rain in the air. My heart soared with hope, the warm, dry morning lifting my spirits higher than they'd ever been during the winter months.

I stepped outside, ready to enjoy the normally arduous task of hanging out a whole family's worth of wet laundry. There wasn't as much as there used to be, since we'd given several items of clothing away over the course of the past few months. We really hadn't needed everything that we had stuffed in our dressers and crammed into our closets. Now we had just enough, and I was grateful for it.

I pulled James' shirt out of the basket at my feet and snapped it in the air once before reaching up to pin it on the clothesline. My hands faltered when I saw the gaunt face of a stranger peering at me from the corner of my house. His eyes were wary, set deep in his head over a jaw full of untrimmed whiskers. He clutched a pack in his arms as tightly as though it were his only salvation.

My heart fluttering at the surprise of seeing him, I asked, "Can I help you?"

He worked his jaw open and shut once without making a sound, then glanced side to side before pinning me with those unnerving eyes of his. "Is this place safe?" he whispered, his voice as rough as a rasp over tree bark.

My heart flooded with compassion, and all traces of fear left me. I knew in an instant, as though someone were speaking it into my mind, that this man needed help, and meant no harm.

"Yes, it's safe."

His shoulders drooped, and his face dipped down once before coming up, his eyes shining with a curious mixture of relief and sorrow.

"Please, come in," I said, abandoning my laundry to lead the way into the kitchen.

"James," I called. "We have a visitor."

When I turned to look behind me, the man was standing just outside the doorway, looking in. He seemed to lack enough courage to cross the threshold.

"If you'd like, you can take a chair by the door," I said. "Leave it open if you want to." I pushed a chair toward him and turned toward my cupboards. "Would you like something to eat?"

"Oh, yes, ma'am," he answered, his voice full of yearning.

James came into the room and extended his hand in greeting. The stranger pulled back, warily eyeing the outstretched hand. Then, in a moment, he straightened up to his full height and returned James' handshake.

"I'm James, and this is my wife, Suzie," James said, pointing to me.

"Happy to meet you," I said, as though we were meeting for a pleasant Sunday dinner instead of being surrounded by the specter of death from a strange disease, no gainful employment in sight, and unsure what disaster the next day might bring.

"I'm Kurt," the stranger said. His eyes cut from James to me and back again. "Have you lived here long?"

"Several years," James said.

"Have you ever been . . . out?"

James sat on a chair opposite Kurt's, which he'd arranged beside the open door. James leaned his elbows on his knees and clasped his hands loosely between them. "What do you mean by *out*?"

"Have you ever been out of this valley? Do you even know what's going on in the world?"

"We have a radio," James said, referring to the crank-generated radio that sat on a table in our bedroom.

"They're liars, you know," Kurt said.

"Who?"

"The radio announcers. They only say what the government tells them to say. They don't say what's real."

James cast a glance my way, and I raised my eyebrows. I pulled out half a loaf of bread, all that remained from the baking I'd done in our woodstove the day before. I cut three crumbly slices and pulled out a can of Spam.

"What is real?" James asked.

Kurt rubbed his eyes, then stared at the floor. "Our country's been invaded."

James sat up straight. "By who?"

"Don't know for sure. Near as I can tell, it's a group of foreign armies," Kurt said. "They wear green and brown camouflage." He gave a short bark of mirthless laughter. "Fat lot of good that does them in the city!"

"What city?"

"They started in the big cities, like New York, about a year ago. Dropped some bombs on any military installations that survived the tornados and volcanoes and things that's been going on, then they sent in their paratroopers. Didn't get much resistance, I can tell you that. Anyone who survived the floods and earthquakes is just trying to find enough to eat."

I carried to Kurt a plate of canned meat and bread, and a bowl of home-canned pears, with a spoon balanced on the bowl's edge. He took the food and set it on his lap, staring down at it as though he wasn't sure what it was.

"I can mix you some powdered milk if you like," I said, wondering a little at his silence.

"This is too much," he said.

"Excuse me?"

"Too much food. I could have fed my whole family with this much, if I'd had it before . . ." Kurt choked on his words and bowed his head.

"Tell us," James insisted, moving his hand toward Kurt in supplication. "We need to know what is happening."

Kurt swallowed a couple of times, then took a slice of bread up in his skeletal fingers. He turned it over and back, then tried a small, reverent bite. He closed his eyes and tilted his face toward Heaven. "Thank you, God," he whispered.

While Kurt ate, he told us more of the invading army. "After they came, it seemed as if they wanted to help us," he said. "They'd heard about all our disasters. They'd had some, too, but I guess not so bad. They stocked our big stores with food, the ones that were still standing, anyway. They were almost like the Red Cross or something. They said we could have whatever we wanted out of their stores, as long as we let them implant a tiny microchip under the skin on the back of our hand." Kurt raised his fist, slashed and spotted with multiple scars, and turned it toward us. "They said it wouldn't hurt. We'd never lose it, and we could get all the food we wanted. It sounded good to me. Their words were sweet, their reasoning sound. If you were robbed of your wallet or purse, you could still get food, because no one could steal your microchip. But we had to have the microchip to get anything from the store."

Kurt stared down at his plate, the food half-eaten. He set the rest aside, and said in a miserable whisper, "My wife didn't want us to take the chip. Said she had a funny feeling. She wanted to keep on bartering for food, as we'd been doing all along. There was this little store around the corner from our house, a place that had been in business since my dad was a little boy." Kurt's mouth twisted up into a ghost of a smile, nostalgia giving us a glimpse of the boy he'd once been. "We went there, because Mr. Robbins didn't insist that we have the chip in our hands to buy anything. He didn't have much, but there were a few suppliers of his that still came through, so we could make do for awhile.

"Then, one day, we went in to get some things, and Mr. Robbins said he was closed. When we asked him why, he said it was because he'd had a visit from a foreign army colonel, telling him it was against the law to sell anything without scanning a microchip embedded in someone's hand. Any place doing business had to use a scanner. Mr. Robbins couldn't afford the technology.

I think they purposely priced it clear out of range because they wanted full control of commerce.

"Mr. Robbins didn't really want to be a part of it—the scanning process, anyway. He said it made his customers more like robots instead of flesh and blood people. So he had to close down. All the surviving independently owned stores closed.

"I tried to convince my wife that the big grocery store had more than enough food. With bartering we were never sure of what or how much we would get. She insisted that bartering was still the best way."

Kurt's face twisted, then crumpled, and he fell silent.

James leaned forward in worry. "What happened?" he asked.

I already knew, the truth of the horror that approached us ever nearer each day unrolling in my mind like an old, mildewed carpet.

Kurt pressed his hands against his face and spoke through his fingers. "She went out to trade, as she'd done so many times before, but this time she didn't come back. The kids were crying for their mama, so I went looking." His voice rose in a thin wail of grief. "They killed her."

James sat up as though he'd gotten an electric shock. "Why?" he asked.

Kurt's shoulders shook in silent grief, unable to answer. I looked at him, my heart reaching out but unsure if I should go over to him or let him work through his own misery.

Trials are to help mankind. The voice was no louder than a whisper in my mind. I didn't bother to look for the speaker, since I knew I would see no one.

Whether we survive the death of loved ones, or lose every earthly thing we have, any experience can pull us closer to our Savior or we can push ourselves away from Him. We can combine forces with Him and thrive, or turn our backs and wallow in grief and self-pity for the rest of our mortal lives, widening the spiritual gap and depriving ourselves of true comfort. If we learn to turn it all over to Father in Heaven, trusting that His will be done, that everything will work out all right in the end, then we can become one of his soldiers for right and truth, helping Him bring to pass miracles and comfort for those on earth.

James reached out and touched Kurt on the knee, a gesture of support.

I turned back to the cupboards and pulled out a large can of powdered milk. I pried off the plastic lid, then opened the canister of chocolate powder, the same canister that I'd dipped into time and again on many frigid nights. It didn't make any sense, but we still had chocolate powder. To all practical minds, it should have been gone months ago. As the winter days rolled by, and we used our food to feed others, we continued to have food to share.

It was as though the scripture story had come to life of the widow who used her last measure of meal and her last drops of oil to make a cake to feed the prophet Elijah, then discovered that she never ran out of food. (1 Kings 17:11-16)

I often thought of the quail and the manna from Heaven sustaining the children of Israel in the desert (Exodus 16:2-18) as well as Christ feeding 5,000 people with only two loaves and five fishes (John 6:5-13). Miracles abound in the scriptures, which are accounts of people very much like us, only in a different time and place.

I never worried anymore about what we were giving out. I figured that if people needed it, then God would provide. And if He didn't, well, then at least we'd all be in the same boat.

Kurt mopped his eyes with a clean dishtowel that James handed him. I carried the cup of chocolate milk over and placed it in his hands, taking the towel and draping it over his knee in case he might want it again. Kurt raised the cup to his lips and took a tentative sip. Then, with eyes closed, he took another small sip, savoring the flavor. He sighed and leaned back in his chair, cradling his cup in both hands.

"Why did they kill your wife?" I asked as gently as I could.

"It turned out that not taking the microchip, or the Mark of the Beast, is unforgivable," Kurt said.

"Bartering means you don't need the chip, so trading for food or anything else was outlawed. Anyone caught disobeying the law is killed without trial, as an example to others. People who refuse to take the microchip are put in labor camps, they and their children, and all of them are forced to work with hardly any food. When the camps are too full, inmates are again offered the choice of taking the microchip or not. If they refuse, they are shot. I was desperate to feed my family, and the chip seemed so insignificant compared to a full belly and children who weren't screaming from hunger. So many of us out there are afraid."

Kurt stared at us with haunted eyes. "They didn't tell us everything at first," he said, his voice low. "After we got used to using the chip, to feeling full, and going to sleep without hearing the cries of our hungry children, they told us that the chip was only the first step. We now were required to take an oath to follow the Crown."

"Whose crown?" James asked.

Kurt shrugged, a defeated gesture. "It's just a word. It means all the countries that have conspired to conquer the United States. They do not believe in God. They forbid any mention of His name in reverence, or anyone saying that Jesus is our Savior. They forbid prayer. Anyone who promises to follow their wicked directives is in very real danger of losing their soul. The devastation is not just to the buildings and streets of the cities. There's a spiritual devastation that these invaders leave in their wake.

"Our nation is crippled. There are many people running from the invading armies, as I have, because if anyone refuses the oath, they're killed, but not outright." Kurt gripped his head in his hands. "They hurt your children first. They kill them slowly right in front of your eyes, when all you'd tried to do was take care of them." Kurt's shoulders quaked, and his voice worked its way out between repressed sobs. "All I wanted to do was to feed my children, that's all." Kurt took in a shuddering breath. "Now they're all dead."

As I watched Kurt rock back and forth, back and forth, trying to deal with his own personal misery, my heart went out to him.

Those who accepted the microchip implant in their hand out of fear were deceived. The Mark of the Beast was not the microchip in their hand, but the devilish oath they had to make in order to save their own mortal life. An oath is a very serious promise, but it's not worth saving your earthly life if you forfeit your eternal one.

CHAPTER SEVEN
Invasion

After Kurt fell into a sleep that seemed as deep as death, James and I talked about the disturbing news he had brought. If what he said was true, the invading armies were sweeping the nation from coast to coast, terrorizing inhabitants, forcing them to take the Mark of the Beast or killing them, usually by beheading, and sticking the heads on a pole in a public place as a warning to anyone who saw them.

Kurt said the citizens were running from the armies, so there would most likely be more people coming, with the enemy not far behind. It was not a pleasant thought.

That night, I had a dream. The city skyline was jagged and crumbled, like a mouth full of rotting teeth. Against the dark backdrop, I could see several fires burning. I could smell the acrid odor of melting rubber and incinerated garbage.

Then I heard terrified, high-pitched screams come

out of the darkness, and the sound of marching feet. I glimpsed a mother picking scraps of food out of a box and pushing them into her mouth. Her two children, mere skeletons, clamored at her side, crying for a bite of food. She grudgingly gave them each a piece of whatever it was she was eating. They wolfed it down, then cried for more, their hands held out toward her in a piteous gesture. She turned the empty box upside down to show them that there was no more.

I saw troops of soldiers in green and brown splotched fatigues, the foliage colors incongruous against the hopeless black of the ruined city as they marched through the streets. These men had no regard for human life.

The soldiers fired their guns at any movement, letting loose bursts of deadly fire, laughing if they got a scream out of a random blast of bullets. When they got bored of shooting, they went hunting for women, to satisfy their animal lusts. I saw acts of cruelty too savage to recount. Unthinkable things happened as I watched.

My heart quailed, and I turned away, sickened, not wanting to see any more. I wanted the whole thing to stop.

Suddenly, I felt a supporting arm around me, a comforting strength that had become familiar only since I'd died and had the chance to stand next to the Savior. _"It is a cleansing. It must happen before I come_ *again."* The simple words brought me comfort.

As if to lighten my heavy heart even more, I was given a glimpse of Paradise, where those spirits who had been suffering in great agony on earth only moments before were freed from their tortured bodies and received into a place of peace and comfort with great rejoicing. Any righteous suffering on earth will be compensated for in Heaven.

I awoke with hope in my heart.

Over the course of the next few weeks, the population of our little town grew greater than the sparse leaves sagging on the trees. Refugees came from all directions, some in rags, some with luggage, some without, all of them hungry. Not all of them stayed very long. Restless of heart and wounded in spirit, Kurt left shortly after he arrived, picking at the scab on the back of his scarred hand as he wandered down the street, his pack perched on his thin shoulders like a vulture. Until he turned his sorrows over to Christ, he would never find the peace he sought.

Ned Chase was one of the newcomers to town. He had a half-grown son at his side, the only other surviving member of his family. The rest had been lost to disease, starvation, or the invading army. Ned's dark eyes looked through to your very soul before darting away to check his surroundings. He missed nothing.

After he'd settled in a tent on our neighbor's back lawn, he began talking to all the able-bodied men in town, first in groups of two or three, then in larger congregations. Ned was itching to go to battle.

After he talked to James about his plans, James discussed them with me.

"People in the cities are too beaten down to defend themselves," he said. "The invaders took the cities easily because of the mass destruction, and because they had the element of surprise. We've been spared a lot of destruction here, and we have guns. If we go to them, they won't be expecting us, and the element of surprise will be on our side."

"So you're going to fight?" I asked.

James gave a single nod. "Yes. We need to defend our country, at least what's left of it. Kyle, Luke, Cody, and Lance are old enough to go with me," he said, naming off our four oldest sons. "We're organizing a company to leave next week."

I examined my feelings, anxious to see what measure of sorrow would undermine my soul, now that I knew my sons and husband were headed for war. Curiously, although I knew I would miss having them with me, I had no fear for their lives. The certainty grew within me that if they kept on the armor of God, as spoken of in Ephesians 6: 11-18, they would be all right. Whether they lived or died, they would be in God's care. There is no greater peace anywhere than knowing that Christ is with us in good or bad times. The Lord will bless us with anything we ask for. If we ask for protection in the

*middle of an attack, the Lord will cloak us with armor.
If we do not want anyone to see us as we are on God's
errand, he will make it so we will not be seen. If we ask
in faith, all things can happen.*

A week later, I waved goodbye to James and our
four grown boys as they left in the company of Ned
and several other able-bodied recruits from Pleasant
View. They took only what they could carry on their
backs, with handguns strapped to their waists and
rifles balanced on their shoulders.

Their departure marked an even greater influx of
refugees. I knew that things were in for a big change
when there were half a dozen families sheltering under
our roof. Some did not even speak English, but we
understood each other anyway. A lot of them had barely
missed the calamities that beset the world outside our
mountain valley. They spoke of being on the outskirts
of the floods, or being shaken by a terrible earthquake.
When the quaking stopped, they went outside their
home only to see their neighbors' houses reduced to
rubble.

As they told me their stories, the Spirit assured me
that certain people were being spared and directed to
various gathering places throughout the earth.

Most came with nothing except a few things in a
purse or pack and empty stomachs. Some had managed
to escape with only their lives, and had the wounds to
show for it. They knew it was only by the mercy of God

that they were not killed or captured, and they were the ones most likely to express deep gratitude for little things, even something as insignificant as a glass of clean water.

I assigned a bedroom or living area to each family so they could have a modicum of privacy. After all those areas were gone, I made room for people to sleep on the floor. All of my children who were still home slept in my bedroom. With all the meals to fix and laundry and cleaning and organizing that went along with having so many people around, I hardly had time to miss James and our boys.

Many of my neighbors sheltered displaced people, too. If not for the help I got from my guests, I could easily have spent my whole day cooking. The people in my house ate in shifts, since there wasn't enough room at the table for all of them at once.

Caroline was one of my houseguests who had come in from Denver, Colorado. After her husband joined the resistance forces to fight the enemy, she stumbled into town in her Nike cross-trainers with her two daughters at her side. In her backpack, she carried cosmetics tucked in among pieces of designer clothing.

At first, she seemed to seek me out nearly every morning. "Oh, Suzanne, I'm so sorry to be troubling you. I hate to take up room in your house. Just as soon as this is all over, I'll pay you. I've got money, I just can't get to it now."

"Caroline, it's no trouble," I said. "And you don't owe me anything. If I had to walk to Denver, I know you'd let me stay with you."

It never quite got through, because the next morning, Caroline would find me and apologize again.

Finally, I said to her, "Look, Caroline, when I was pregnant with my twins, I got so big, so fast, that I couldn't do it all. If I got up and moved around, I would go into premature labor. I had to have help in order for my babies to survive. People even had to help me feed my family. It was hard. Sometimes I felt like I owed so much to all those people who washed my family's dirty laundry and vacuumed my floors. But feeling bad about the help they gave me was prideful on my part."

"I guess that is how I am feeling," Caroline said, looking at the floor.

I touched her arm and said, "I finally realized those people were being blessed for helping me. There's no way I can give back to all those people who gave to me when I needed it, but I can give what I have to the Lord now. Everything I have has always been His. He's the one who's giving to you and everyone else who's staying here."

I reached out and gave Caroline a hug. When we pulled apart, there were tears in her eyes. "You are welcome here, for as long as you need to stay," I said. "No apologies. It's your house as much as it is mine.

I just happened to move in first."

After a moment, Caroline spoke. "I never really knew my neighbors in Denver," she said. "We'd wave if we saw one another, but I don't even recall their names. Yet I feel so close to everyone here." Her eyes widened, and she gave a little laugh. "I don't mean how closed in we are, I mean, close . . . emotionally. I wouldn't trade the company of anybody in this house for anyone I knew before."

We are taught from childhood that it is better to give than to receive, so having to receive help from anyone will be hard for many of the good people.

One morning, I awoke with a warning flowing through my body that made my hair stand on end and my nerves go tight. I knew we had to leave immediately.

Just as the stories in the scriptures where people were warned of danger in time to escape, such as Joseph taking Mary and Jesus to Egypt when King Herod declared that all baby boys were to be killed (Matthew 2:13), Lot (Genesis 19:29) and other prophets who were told in a vision or dream in the middle of the night of danger, we were being warned that it was time to depart from our town.

We had to go deep into the mountains. All of us. The enemy was coming.

CHAPTER EIGHT
Change of Address

I cinched the straps on Joseph's pack. Although my youngest son was nearly as tall as me, it was hard for me to accept that he was as old as he was. I swept my gaze over my remaining children. They all shouldered packs, each one carrying a single change of clothing, topped with a blanket or sleeping bag to guard against the nights we'd be spending in the mountains. I was pretty sure we wouldn't be coming back to Pleasant View.

For the first time since they left, I worried about James and our boys. What if they came back here and found us gone? What would they do? Would they wait for us to come back, or go looking for us? How would they ever find us? I couldn't even leave them a message, since I didn't know myself where we were going.

Finally, I realized I just had to put my trust in the Lord.

Although others had premonitions that we should

leave, and they helped me warn everyone in town that the enemy army was coming, not everyone wanted to go. They were either afraid to leave their homes to live in the mountains, or else they felt they had something else they were supposed to do before they left. Perhaps they felt the need to stay and defend the town. That was nothing I could decide for them, as God grants every one of us free agency, underlined by Christ's atonement. Every man is responsible to make whatever decision is right for him.

One thing I do know is that some people are emotionally attached to inanimate objects. If their hearts are set on their possessions, then when they finally decide to tear themselves away from them, it may be too late. This is when fear comes. If we are attached to any earthly thing and not to God, we cannot make it. We all know that we can't take anything with us when we die. It will be the same in the Last Days. Those who just cannot leave their homes will see the worst of the worst. We cannot hold onto anything but our families. That's what's most important. The Lord will provide the rest.

Our leader was Scott Davidson, a red-haired man, his temples streaked with gray. Although Scott was not a local resident, he knew about surviving in the wilderness. He had come into our valley from Arizona, where he had seen the invading army, their foliage fatigues standing out against the brown of desert.

He was all for avoiding them, outwitting them and outsmarting them.

There were about 250 people in our company. We had a group prayer, then headed to the mountains on foot. The four-wheelers sat idle in backyards, useless without gas. No one in town had horses anymore. They'd either died or had been let loose to forage the best they could when their feed ran out.

Anyone who had built a bomb shelter had to leave it behind. Building bomb shelters is acting out of fear. Having excessive food storage, to the point of fanaticism, is also prompted by fear, and fear can attract destruction.

A few people pulled deer carts—contraptions with one large wheel that could maneuver on rough terrain. They were originally designed to get a deer carcass out of the mountains more easily than dragging it, but they worked just as well to carry heavier gear, such as pots and pans. Some pulled children's wagons along behind them. Several die-hard teenagers started out on bicycles with saddlebags of provisions fastened behind their seats. Some pulled and pushed various types of trailers that had been used for hauling wood or trips to the dump in their former lives. Now they were vehicles for survival.

In spite of leaving so much behind, the general mood of our party was one of joy and eager anticipation.

Things are replaceable. Eternity is not.

Just as we slipped into the foothills, we heard the unfamiliar hum of motors and felt the vibration of the earth beneath our feet. Scott told us to stand still, because the invading army was near. We obeyed.

The army marched right past us, so close we could hear their footfalls. We could even see them, their voices sounding across the mountainside in a foreign language that was hard to identify. We were not hidden, yet they didn't notice us. Not one of them even glanced our way.

For two days, we were as quiet as we knew how to be and still make our way further into the heart of the mountains.

We combined our personal food storages into one that anyone could draw upon.

As we traveled, lived, and worked together, it seemed that the food was a nearly endless supply, as it had been in my home when I shared it with others. The same thing had happened to others in town, proving that if you have a single piece of bread left in your house, and a hungry person comes to your door, you will be blessed beyond any of your expectations if you will share what you have with anyone in need.

There were those I encountered, even while living in Pleasant View, who saw things differently. They felt that the food they had stored was only for them. They quoted the scripture about the ten virgins waiting for the bridegroom (Matthew 25:1-12). They insisted that since they were prepared, they would be the ones to benefit from their foresight, and whoever had not prepared must suffer their own fate.

Yet more than once, I saw these people cut open their sealed food containers only to find creepy crawlies in it, like weevils or worms. Often, pulling off the lid was accompanied by a horrible smell of rot and decay. When this happened, it was usually so bad, they had to throw out the whole bucket of wheat or sugar or beans or whatever it was they had planned to fix for their own private meal. If it happened while they were still living in their house, they had to open the windows, regardless of the weather outside, to air out the room. It reminded me of the Israelites who hoarded manna when they were told not to. (Exodus 16:20)

Interestingly enough, when these tight-fisted people would come asking for food from those who had open hearts and hands, they would receive their portion of soup or bread, and then recoil. To them, the odor of the wholesome food was the same as the food that they had found mysteriously rotting in their own supplies. Yet no one else who was eating noticed a strange odor, and went on with their meal, happy with their portion and nourished by its simple goodness.

If those who hoarded their supplies got the message and prayed for forgiveness, then the next day, all was well and they were able to eat.

If they didn't learn their lesson, then they would

never learn it, and they would ultimately not be strong enough to make it.

You must know that it is important that we prepare ourselves temporally. We cannot spend all our time saying, "The Lord will provide" and do nothing for ourselves. It is not pleasing to the Lord if we expect to live on handouts from others when we are capable of doing useful work ourselves. It takes prayer and keeping ourselves out of fear to know how to prepare. There are many good guides available, and bit by bit is usually the most effective method. Most importantly, we should keep an open communication with Father in Heaven and seek for understanding, then do whatever you can to get ready. We cannot make it all alone, but we need to do all we can.

After we'd been on the trail for a few days, I noticed two girls sitting by the side of the road, pulling off their shoes.

I stopped, and my children gazed down at the girls with curiosity. "What are you doing?" I asked.

One girl with blonde braids glanced up. "Emily has blisters from her shoes, so we're trading."

"Aren't you afraid you'll get blisters?" I asked.

The girl cocked her head. "No, I never thought of that." She glanced over at Emily. "But I'm trading anyway. Then we'll both wear band aids, right, Emily?"

I smiled and moved on, remembering the same kind of selfless love I'd seen in my twin boys when they were little. If they had a donut to share, one would break it in two, then give the larger piece to his brother, keeping the smaller one for himself.

While moving through the mountains, we camped outdoors, not bothering with our tents as we tried to avoid the enemy. We huddled together in quiet family groups under a pile of blankets, quilts, and sleeping bags. I usually stayed awake for a while at night, listening, as my children's breathing grew steady and deep, and I contemplated the eternal stars and our uncertain future.

CHAPTER NINE

Spiritual Gifts

Over time, I was witness to many spiritual gifts bestowed on people who did not fear man. Christ beams with joy whenever he sees people doing great acts of kindness for their fellowman. When we know Christ is at our side, we can do anything, for fear is not of God.

Gifts of the Spirit will be strong while living through the Last Days. Having the Spirit of God with us is a gift, for without it there would be no influence except from the devil. We cannot wait for others to tell us what to do. Even with our leaders in place, the day-to-day decisions we must make are vital. We have to be able to hear and act on spiritual promptings at a moment's notice.

The gift of discernment is so vital, it's the first gift we should seek. There will always be deceivers. Even in the scriptures, it says that the very elect may be deceived. (Mark 13:22) We must pray to see beyond the outward appearance or persuasive words, pray that we will not be deceived.

The gift of sight goes along with the gift of discernment. It is the ability to see angels walking with you as plainly as if they had flesh, and since the adversary can and will pose as something good if he thinks that he can ensnare someone by doing so, you need discernment to know what you are seeing. Thinking we cannot be deceived is the devil's plan. Go with what you feel, not just what you see.

Another gift related to discernment is that of being able to understand what is being taught. After discernment comes understanding. Sometimes we get an answer we do not like. It takes time to understand why the Lord has us go through certain trials. When we have a gift of perfect understanding, of being able to see the big picture from beginning to end, we also realize a great gift of comfort.

The gift of comfort is a companion to the Gift of the Holy Spirit. He is the first comforter, testifying that the Lord is our Savior. This can be the very beginning of our spiritual gifts, if that is what we wish, because if we pray for comfort, we will receive it.

The gift of prophecy is more than just telling the future. It is also testifying that the Lord lives. Telling the future is not dangerous if it is of God.

In fact, it can save the lives of those who will listen. The agency of others is never in question. This is quite different from fortune telling, where people ask, "What should I do? What will happen in my future?" without even thinking to ask God. The practice of seeking to have our fortunes told is, in effect, giving our agency to another—the fortuneteller. Instead, we must take responsibility for ourselves.

The true gift of prophecy would be like receiving a warning of impending danger in a dream or vision. It's a great comfort to know that we can be forewarned in time to be led out of danger. The situation may be small enough to only affect family or close friends. No matter how small it may seem, when you receive a spiritual prompting, act on it. This is not fortune telling, this is inspiration.

The gift of tongues is the ability to speak or understand a different language when needed.

The gift of faith is knowing that the Lord will guide us and teach us in times of need, knowing that our prayers will be answered, that we will be provided for, that all is well and we will be led to what we should do. Faith can move mountains. (Matthew 21:21)

The gift of healing means that men and women who have it can know how to help someone just by looking at them. They will be able to touch someone who is afflicted and the sick one will be healed of their illness or injury. When appointed by God, in rare occasions they are even able to raise the dead.

The only way to make it through troubled times is to not worry about yourself. Devote your thoughts and energy to others. Don't care if you live or die or get blisters on your heels. Certainly, do all you can to resolve any dilemma you may find yourself in, then trust God with the rest. Fear brings in bad things, while faith brings good. We cannot make it without the Lord. If we do not think of Him often, we will starve. If we die helping another, the glory is great and our suffering is done.

An important characteristic we must possess to use a spiritual gift is humility. If we begin to be prideful and feeling we are better than others, our ability to use these gifts will be taken away. If we are humble, the Lord is able to work through us in ways that aren't possible if we are filled with pride.

We all need to work together in hard times to make it. There can be no selfishness in our souls if we are to see Christ when He comes again.

CHAPTER TEN

Valley of Peace

As we traveled, moving ever deeper into the sheltering mountains, the summer gave way to autumn, and we added several new people to our ranks along the way.

Some were single stragglers who fled the incoming armies, seeking relief from the constant threat of capture and torture. Some were warned in dreams that they should leave and seek refuge in the mountains. I got an impression of the Lord whispering in their ears, telling them to leave, and where they should go.

We must be able to hear when it's time to listen. If we do not hear or know His voice, then we may not make it.

Many people we came across left their homes in the middle of the night, not telling anyone where they were headed. Others we encountered were in small family groups. Some groups weren't families, but were made up of people who had found each other and banded together. As we were the largest group, we invited everyone to join us. Some did, but others did not.

We'll be comfortable where we fit in, where there are others who think along the same lines that we do. Think if it this way; you probably wouldn't be comfortable wearing a sweat suit to a formal dance.

People seek their own kind, matching minds and souls. In this quiet gathering process I saw going on, the religion you come from doesn't matter. Loving Christ is the only common denominator. The way to worship may be a bit different, but those of the same thoughts and feelings come together anyway, the givers with the givers.

Having a relationship with the Lord is what matters. The selfless find each other, and the selfish either stay by themselves, not trusting anyone, or stay with their select little group, refusing to join forces with people they don't know. It can be compared to the outlook of a thief, who thinks that everyone is a thief simply because he is one himself. He trusts no one.

It was heartening to recognize little miracles happening everywhere. When one of the little boys lost the top button off his coat, it was found along the trail after a short search. One of the older men in our company slipped while chopping wood, and the axe fell hard against his shoe, slicing the leather open. But his foot was whole. When we needed something, be it a vegetable peeler that no one remembered packing or a child's lost toy, after a prayer and a brief search, it would be there.

With early autumn frost nipping at our heels, Scott finally led us into a nearly hidden mountain valley that sheltered a stream of cold water.

We set up tents in the valley, dug latrines, and organized ourselves, dividing up duties according to what each one was able to do. Our group didn't just magically get along when we were first thrown together. We had to feel our way through which attitudes worked and which ones didn't. We had to learn to let go of our attachment to our own "things."

We soon discovered that if people in our group didn't cooperate, it was hard to find enough food for everyone. The hunters weren't successful. But if everyone was getting along and caring for one another, then wild game all but walked up to the hunters, and we enjoyed plenty to eat. When we cheerfully shared and were patient with one another, we found berries of all kinds, juicy and sweet enough to make syrup without sugar. But if we were contentious, the bushes would be bare or only offer us sour, shriveled fruit.

We women got rather creative with cooking. We'd dig a pit and build a fire in the bottom, then when the coals were good and hot, we'd put pots of food inside and cover them up. They'd cook with the least amount of firewood possible. Our pressure cookers worked great when used this way. Since pressure cookers are already famous for cooking food rather quickly and sealing in moisture, it seemed that no matter what kind of meat was brought into camp, whatever was pressure-cooked came out tender. Where a pot of beans would normally take four or five hours to cook, when we cooked them in the pressure cooker underground, they'd be done in an hour or so.

One day, in the early winter, when new snow lay on the frozen ground, my son Joseph pushed aside our tent flap and came in without his coat on.

"Joseph?" I asked. "Where did you leave your coat?"

He tossed his head toward the tent opening. "You know the Pettingills?"

I nodded. The family had come in a couple of weeks ago, having walked all the way from Texas, burying two children along the way.

"Well, their kid didn't have a coat, and he was cold, so I gave him mine."

"Joseph!"

"It's okay, Mom. I'm used to snow, and he's not. Besides, I just don't feel cold." He grabbed a cracker from the stack of homemade ones I had sitting in our tent.

"I need to take a turn grinding wheat," Joseph said. "See you later." Then he ducked back out into the weak winter sunlight.

I needn't have worried about my son. Not only was

this winter not nearly as cold as the previous one, but it seems that Joseph's selflessness cloaked him in the warmth of the Lord. It probably helped, too, that he was frequently called upon to operate one of the hand wheat grinders, which burned calories and boosted his own body heat.

Cooking for so many people took a lot of effort and time, but some of us enjoyed the task. The food was kept in a united tent, and those of us who liked cooking took turns. Others preferred to clean up after the meals. There were others who liked to sew, and some who liked to teach and care for the children. Some were natural organizers, seeing that all the camp tasks were performed smoothly. Those who liked to work with rock were directed to build rock fireplaces and ovens to be used inside the tents, so we could have greater warmth for the winter. Some came up with ways to more easily live without electricity. Some liked to hunt, some to chop wood, others were storytellers or entertainers.

Without pride or selfishness, our tent city operated smoothly through the winter, and we were happy. Our children built snow caves, delighting in the discovery of warmth inside a shelter made of ice. The woodchoppers had good-natured contests, which were great fun to watch, and made the woodcutters doubly warm. We even had babies born in our tent city, and they were all delivered safely.

One cold evening, we were surprised to see a man stagger through the frozen brush with an infant in his arms and three children hanging onto his coat. In spite of their warm coats and boots, the children's lips were tinged light purple from cold as the sun slipped behind the mountain, their cheeks buffed red from the freezing winds. The baby looked to be not more than a week old, his fingers buried in his tiny mouth, his eyes squeezed shut behind paper-thin lids while his tiny jaw tried to work milk out of his dry fist.

When the man caught sight of us, he stopped, his mouth open and wordless with shock. Then he lifted the little bundle in his arms. "My baby needs food," he said. "My wife died giving birth . . ." He broke down sobbing. Scott hurried to his side and put his arm around him.

My friend Stacey was the next one to reach him. She took the infant, saying, "I'll take care of him," then disappeared into her tent to nurse the hungry little boy. Jillian was over a year old by now, and was nearly weaned, although Stacey still nursed her once or twice a day.

The man said his name was Greg, and he and his children were welcomed into our tent city. Stacey took over the feeding and general care of the infant, Porter, who soon grew fat and happy.

It was actually good for Stacey to have something to occupy her time besides Jillian, since her husband had gone off to fight in the war with the other men from Pleasant View.

When spring arrived, so did more people, bringing news of fresh horrors from the outside world.

Parents were killing their children, either from neglect or through acts of violence. Some mothers abandoned their children to starve. Some parents killed their babies outright, or laid them on the ground and just walked away. Some justified these actions by saying they couldn't provide for their children, so it was better that they die swiftly.

That decision is best left to God. There are many people who have used childhood hardships as a springboard for tremendous adult spiritual strength. Sometimes the strength derived from childhood hardships has a great impact for good on other people's lives.

Children were also killing their parents. More and more people out in the world were concerned solely with self-preservation. Yet many others found the struggle for life too hard, and ended it by suicide.

If people would only rely on the Lord, He could work miracles in their lives.

Many who came in to settle with us said that our tent city had a faint glow, as if a protective bubble had settled over our valley.

Some reported stopping briefly in other tent cities, places where people were suspicious or unfriendly. They reported dirty conditions, no organization, children fighting and arguing, general lack of food, although some of the inhabitants appeared to be better fed than others.

Out of necessity, they would sometimes stay a night with these groups of people, but it was with an uneasy heart because everyone acted afraid that others were going to take their things. They guarded their own food all night long. If they slept, they could wake up to find themselves with absolutely nothing, and no one willing to share.

There were reports of marauding bands of survivors, not associated with the invading army, but bent on stealing. Generally, these were bands of men who would storm into a tent city and take whatever they wanted, usually food, before disappearing back into the undergrowth.

Others said they stumbled upon camps that asked them what religion they professed. If they did not name the correct religion, whichever one the tent city inhabitants shared, they were turned away.

As before, some of the newcomers chose not to stay with us. Our combined happiness seemed to drive some people nuts. In spite of our reassurances that they were welcome, some people left quietly in the night. If they moved on in the daylight, we sent them with food and our heartfelt wishes for them to find a place where they would be happy.

The gathering of God's people will happen naturally, like when we make friends, we find people with whom we are most comfortable to hang around with. It's a natural selection process. It can even be compared to Noah gathering animals for the ark. (Genesis 7:8,9) Noah didn't have to go out with a net and ropes to build traps to catch all the animals. They were moved upon by the Lord to gather at the ark, and Noah organized the boarding process.

That's what this gathering of people felt like to me, that individuals were directed to where they should go in order to match those of like minds and hearts.

One day, a couple of people who'd stayed behind in Pleasant View when we'd moved into the mountains the year before found our camp. They were thin and nervous, looking around as though they expected some horror to jump out from behind every tree. "What happened to you?" I asked, rushing over to greet them as soon as I recognized who they were.

"The army came," one said. "They took over the town, beat and killed anyone who offered resistance, and took our food. We barely escaped."

My heart was heavy for those who had been left behind, but buoyed with gratitude for the relative safety we'd found in the valley. The righteous will not miss every disaster that visits the earth. Yet if we have faith in all areas of our life, we can be saved from most of the hardships to come.

Besides funneling in straggling refugees, one day the canyon walls that led to our encampment echoed with the voices of men speaking a foreign tongue. People who'd heard that language before stiffened with fear. "It's them, it's the enemy!" they hissed.

Scott called a couple of men to his side, and they headed out of the valley, toward the sound of voices. After awhile, the two men came racing back. Without explanation, they scooped up a couple of blankets and some food, then dashed away again.

A half hour later, Scott and the men returned. We were full of questions.

"There were some men in fatigues, wearing boots and carrying rifles over their shoulders. They wanted warm bedding and food," Scott said.

"How did you know that?" someone asked. "Do you speak their language?"

"Not any more," Scott said. "It was through the gift of tongues that I understood them. I didn't want them to see our camp, so I sent back for the things they wanted and kept the soldiers occupied. They seemed happy to wait, telling me tales of their adventures in America. If I'd not been able to understand them, I'm afraid they would have overpowered us and come into our valley. Then they could have taken over, maybe even killed us."

We offered a prayer of gratitude for our safety right there and then. The next Sunday, we dedicated our service to gratitude for God's tender mercies. We held our church meeting under the trees. It was shady and pleasant, with the sound of the stream a musical backdrop for the scripture reading and prayers. We prayed in gratitude for the Lord cloaking our city, making it invisible to our enemies and keeping us safe. We enjoyed great peace, and we all truly cared for one another.

It didn't take long for us to learn that putting away our pride made our primitive living conditions like a piece of Heaven on earth. We all focused more on the Lord's coming than our current circumstances, and we all knew in our hearts that anything we were required to go through would be worth it when we could meet Christ face to face, to touch the prints in his hands, knowing what He went through for us. It would all be worth it in the end.

CHAPTER ELEVEN

Into Harm's Way

Scott stood before us after our church meeting, holding his silence until the entire congregation quieted. Then he said, "It's time to move."

We turned to stare at one another, surprise evident on some faces, a knowing look on others.

My own heart beat with anticipation. New Jerusalem had to be built before Christ would come again, and I knew that's where we were headed.

In the morning, we packed up again, this time in handcarts that had been built during the long days of winter camp from parts of bicycles and old trailers. There were even some made with wooden wheels. The abundant deadfall trees in the valley around us supplied the building materials. The handcarts proved sturdy and easy to maneuver through the rough mountain trails, plus they carried more gear than a bicycle.

I felt a twinge of nostalgia for our beautiful mountain valley that had sheltered us for so long. There were those who talked of staying behind, but I knew it was only sentiment. Now that it had been decided, I was anxious to move on.

The children ran ahead in their eagerness to see what surprises lay ahead, the older people measuring their pace so they would have sufficient energy to finish out the day.

When we stopped to make camp in the evening, I went looking for Stacey, but I couldn't find her anywhere. My sense of unease grew when I asked Greg if he'd seen her, and he told me that Porter was missing, too. I found Jillian safe in the care of another lady who had a little girl about her same age.

Before I could report the situation to Scott, he had already started backtracking with five other armed men, including Greg, who was anxious to find his missing son. The rest of us knelt and prayed for the success of their mission.

By the time we had supper ready, they still weren't back. We fed the children, but the rest of us agreed to fast for our party's safe return.

After the children were tucked into their sleeping bags and blankets, we heard footsteps heading toward us from the back trail. With great relief, we welcomed the scouting party, with Stacey and Porter in their midst.

Stacey collapsed onto the ground, and someone brought her a generous plate of food.

The searchers got in line to get some supper, including Greg, who had a dozing Porter tucked into his shoulder.

"Let me hold him so you can eat," I said, gently taking hold of the baby.

"Thanks." Greg surrendered his son, and I carried him over to Stacey.

"What happened?" I asked, rocking Porter in my arms.

"I couldn't get Porter to stop fussing, so I moved a little way off the trail and sat down on a rock to nurse him," Stacey said. "I thought he would get finished and fall asleep so that I could catch up and everything would be fine. But he seemed to have a tummy ache or something, and was squirming all over the place."

I glanced down at the sleeping baby in my arms. "He seems to have gotten over it," I said.

"Yeah, but you should have seen him this afternoon. I kept at it, trying to burp him, then feed him, then burp him again.

"After awhile, I heard footsteps, then voices. At first I was relieved, thinking that someone from our group had missed me and came back to help. But then I realized the voices were speaking the enemy's language." Stacey stopped and pressed one hand against her chest. "I nearly fainted. I was so scared. There was no place to hide, and there was no time to run away. Porter was fussing as much as ever, crying louder than ever. The only thing I could think to do was pray, and it was a fast one. Just 'Oh, Heavenly Father, please help us.'"

Stacey wiped her eyes with the back of her hand. "Those soldiers walked right past us, with just a bush between them and us. Not a single one of them paused or even stopped talking to one another. It was as if Heaven put earplugs on them or something. It was amazing. I thanked Father in Heaven over and over, but I was too scared to move until the search party came to get us."

That wasn't the last brush we had with enemy soldiers. They had moved into the mountains right behind the refugees. At times, our scouts would see a stranger, and would feel a warning to go no closer. We discovered that the army would sometimes send their soldiers out dressed as travelers, searching for the cities in the mountains, hunting the people who had escaped their iron rule. I was sure that Scott's pronouncement to move out of our valley had come none too soon.

One evening, our hunting party came back with a man who was bloody and bruised. He had a hard time keeping on his feet, even though he was supported on both sides by our strongest men. He was a victim of the enemy, and had been left for dead, which he most likely would have been by morning if our hunters hadn't brought him back to camp. His name was Walker.

We bandaged his wounds and gave him food. After

a night's sleep, he awoke the next morning with news for us.

"The cities are getting worse," Walker said. "The wicked grow more wicked with each passing day. But those who believe in Christ are strengthening their belief. Some will share their last piece of dried bread with a stranger, believing that the Lord will provide for their families. Yet they must do it in great secrecy, for the wicked are out in great force, their hearts filled with hatred, turning any compassion they might have once had to bitter ash. They take prisoners now, as they did me. They are no longer merely content with murder, but now find more pleasure in maiming people than killing them outright, leaving them to live in greater misery than before."

Walker's words rang true. Our real selves do not come out until we are tried and tested. We may not even know ourselves what we are made of until we are faced with trials so severe that we are either broken or strengthened by the event. We grow more from pain and hardship than when things are easy.

Walker was a man who believed in and loved the Lord. He told us that a lot of people who'd fled the city were living in shantytowns, crude structures built out of anything they could find, from cardboard boxes to sheets of rusty tin.

"They guard their belongings at all times, even at night," Walker said. "If they happen to fall asleep at the wrong time, they're apt to wake up with nothing, not even the shanty over their heads. They may even lose a body part or two."

It was my turn to change Walker's bandages. I pulled the blood-soaked dressing from his head and stared at the wicked gash underneath, where skin had been peeled from his skull. It looked as though they'd scalped him while he was still alive.

"Does it still hurt?" I asked.

"Whatever happens to me in this life doesn't matter," Walker said. "Life is short."

He winced as I placed a fresh dressing over his wound.

"Don't get me wrong, I'm glad you rescued me and all," Walker said. "But even if I'd died at the hands of my enemies, it wouldn't have mattered. If I'm more concerned about 'what do I want?' instead of what the Lord wants me to do, then what difference would it make if I lived or died? I'd rather not have to keep working on all those things I can easily learn here, like obedience and faith, so should I be more worried about what happens to me here, or what happens in the next life?"

I finished taping the dressing down, and Walker gave me a smile of gratitude.

"Yet, it appears that God would have me stay alive for now," he said. Then he closed his eyes and surrendered to sleep.

CHAPTER TWELVE

Angels Among Us

When we moved on the next day, Walker went with us. When we stopped for our mid-day rest, he glanced around at the mountains that surrounded us, then said, "There are many people in these mountains. Besides the armies and refugees, there are those who have been sent from Heaven. Angels are testing people on earth. I've seen them dressed as beggars, asking for money or food. Many people pass them by without a glance. There are those who even speak disparagingly of them, calling them 'filthy beggars,' and worse. The test is to see who has compassion and a righteous heart."

Walker's story reminded me of a time when some homeless men came to me, saying that their families were hungry and they needed money to buy food. I had no money, since I'd just used all I had to buy groceries, so I offered them some of the food I'd just bought.

"No," one of them said. "The bread would get mashed in our packs. We need money."

I had no money. Since they refused what I had to offer, I went on my way, doubtful that they even had a hungry family.

Yet it wasn't for me to judge. If I feel I should help someone, and give them money, after which they go out to buy beer and get themselves drunk, then so what? It's their choice on what they do with the money. My responsibility ends when I decide whether or not I'm going to help others with whatever I can give at that time.

Walker seemed to have read my thoughts, because the next thing he said was, "Help those less fortunate than you however you can. They may not be angels, but they are God's children. They could very well stand in judgment of us at the final bar of God. I don't want to hear anyone tell God that I called him names or kicked dirt on him.

"Even if the Spirit prompts you to do the smallest thing, do it. You may never know how your actions may bless a lot of lives. Do not question. Just act.

"There are men on the Lord's errand who are not only here to gather the righteous, but are also here to take care of those who have faith. If humble people need food, or medicine, or any other thing, and ask for it in righteousness, these men will see that they get whatever they need."

Greg's head flew up, and his eyes bored into Walker. "What do these men look like?"

Walker gave Greg a knowing grin. "Just like you and me. Why?"

"My wife, when we left Missouri, I knew she was due to have Porter any time, but we couldn't stay. No one could, and live. The invading army was too close. The only thing we could do was join the band of survivors escaping westward. Sylvia knew it was the only thing we could do. But when we hit the mountains, she was all done in. It was too much for her to carry the baby and keep going.

"The rest of our group had to go on. They traveled at night so the army wouldn't see them. I knew it was selfish, no, impossible to expect them to stay with us, but I also knew I couldn't leave Sylvia. I stayed behind with her, me and the kids, and built a crude shelter out of branches. Not long afterward, she had Porter. Then she just let go of life and slipped away from me.

"She was so pretty. When she died, all the worry lines were gone from her face, and she looked just like the girl I proposed to ten years ago." Greg stopped and lifted his gaze up to the top of a nearby tree, his mind lost in the past.

"Then what?" Walker asked gently.

"It was too cold to bury her," Greg said. "I was exhausted, both emotionally and physically, and I had no shovel to dig with. All I could do was wrap her up in the blanket she'd given birth to Porter on and put her body up in a tree. My little ones sat watching me, unmoving, their faces so sad and tired. As soon as I had done all I could for Sylvia, I knew I had to get the children moving, or they would freeze.

"They were so unnaturally still, and I didn't want them mourning their mother to the point that they would just give up and die, too. I had to carry Porter, and I managed to boost my youngest daughter up onto my hip, but the other two had to hold onto my coat and walk.

"It was getting dark, and we had no place to go. Our tent and all of our meager belongings had gone ahead with our company. I wondered if we might be able to catch up to them before we starved to death, because we'd eaten all our food.

"It was hard going through the snow, and I was soon mired in despair. I wondered if it wouldn't have been better for all of us to die along with Sylvia.

"Then one of my children said through chattering teeth, 'Daddy, should we say a prayer?' The faith of a child was enough to bring me to my senses, and remind me that I hadn't yet called upon God for help. We stopped and prayed.

"As soon as we said, 'Amen,' a few men came walking out from between the trees, carrying lanterns. They were cheerful men, dressed in warm coats and each one carried a blanket that they wrapped around one of my older children, then lifted them up into their arms. I kept hold of Porter, and followed as they led the way to a nice, warm house right there in the mountains. It wasn't part of any resort that I could see. It seemed to be all by itself. I thought it was an odd place to live, but I wasn't about to refuse their help.

"Going inside that warm building was like entering Heaven. They gave us food, and had enough beds and blankets for all of us to sleep warmly. They even had milk for Porter.

"After a few days, I felt like a new man. They gave us all coats. I didn't stop to wonder at the time why they would have clothes to fit children when there were no children around besides my own. They gave us all boots, too. Then they told me which direction to travel, and I set off, as if I was compelled to go. At the time, it didn't seem strange in the least that I wanted to leave.

"But then, just when I began wondering what I'd been thinking to leave a warm cabin and press on with my children in the mountains in winter, I stumbled across this group."

Walker gave Greg a grin. "You were helped, all right. The faith of your little children brought those that are anxious and waiting to help right to your side. And don't you doubt it for a minute. A lot of people don't even know that men of God, or angels, are helping them." Walker gave Greg a conspiratorial wink. "You do."

Greg nodded, his eyes wet. "I still can't love those

who forced us to the wilderness in the first place. They killed my Sylvia."

"Turn them over to God," Walker said. "They will receive the reward they deserve."

"I'd would rather hear more cheerful things tonight," I said.

Walker stopped speaking and looked over at me for a moment. Then, with a twinkle in his eye, he pushed himself to his feet. "Okay," he said with a smile. "How about, 'It's time to move on.'"

CHAPTER THIRTEEN
Slippery Cliff

When we crested the final mountain, we saw the plains spread out before us, like a superhighway compared to the difficult mountain passes we had traveled through. Our spirits soared. Some of us raised our arms and gave a loud cheer, jumping with delight.

When I quit dancing around, I had to hike up the waistband of my pants. I'd lost a little weight while hiking through the mountains.

Our descent was unsteady, because of loose rocks and the steep grade we had to travel. I was on a handcart toward the back of the column, finding my way down a narrow passage with rock walls on either side, digging my feet into the ground to keep the handcart from running over me, when Caroline stopped her cart in front of me. I nearly ran into it, but managed to hold back.

"What's wrong?" I asked.

Caroline glanced over her shoulder with confusion

in her eyes as she struggled to hold her own cart steady. "I don't know."

Word soon came back along the line that there had been a serious accident. We slowly worked our way forward until the rock wall on the right fell away to a steep drop-off. It was slightly wider here, but there still wasn't enough room for us to assemble.

I saw some of the men in our company standing at the edge of the drop-off, glancing over the side with somber faces. One of them was Greg.

"What happened?" I asked Greg.

"Scott fell," he said.

"Oh, no!" I instinctively moved toward the edge of the cliff to look.

"No," Greg said, his hand shooting out to warn me off. "You don't need to see this."

"But he needs help!" I said.

"Walker and some others have already gone down there to retrieve his body."

I stared at Greg, realization dawning as a river of sick apprehension ran through me. "His body? You don't mean he's..."

Greg shrugged, but his eyes told me what I didn't want to hear. "I don't know for sure. I only know that after they got down to him, he quit hollering all of a sudden."

I turned away from the precipice and moved forward, my throat tight and my heart aching. I know that those who die while in the service of the Lord are in good hands, but in spite of what I knew, tears started rolling down my face. Even though Scott was a good man, and worthy of a great reward, I was pained to think that he may no longer be among us.

A little further along the trail, a meadow broadened out, and I saw that everyone who'd been ahead of me had pulled off the path and were facing the trail, waiting and watching with somber faces for further developments. I joined them.

When the last handcart came into view, a couple of men walked on either side of it, holding onto a still figure draped over the top. Although the figure's head was half-covered with a bloody bandage, and one arm and a leg wore crude splints made of narrow tree limbs tied with torn shirt strips, I recognized Scott lying there, so limp and lifeless. My hand flew to my mouth as I stifled a sob. A silent prayer rose up from my soul, begging for comfort and understanding.

The handcart stopped as soon as the trail leveled out. The men lifted Scott off the makeshift hearse as one of the women threw a blanket on the ground. Scott was lowered gently onto the blanket before the men removed their hats.

"He was still breathing when we got to him," one of the men said. He worked his hat brim between his fingers. "But it is hard to tell now."

"This is no one's fault," another man said in a voice

firm enough to discourage contradiction. "God is over all."

"Please, everyone," Walker said, his voice solemn. "Let us pray."

We all bowed our heads, and Walker offered up a prayer with words that washed my heart with peace and comfort. I knew that all was well.

After the "Amen," Walker glanced at the men around him. They nodded, as though they had reached a decision among themselves without even needing to speak. Greg and Walker knelt beside Scott's still form. They laid their hands on his head and prayed over Scott, saying that he was still needed on earth, that with his faith he would be healed. Their words were so powerful that a prickle went down my spine.

No sooner had Walker closed the blessing in the name of Jesus Christ than Scott stirred, sat up, and blinked in confusion at all the faces surrounding him. He raised his splinted arm. "What's going on?" he asked.

Walker gave Scott a friendly thump on the back. "Time to get back to work," he said with a laugh.

The men removed the splints from Scott's limbs, the same arm and leg that had been snapped in two when he fell down the mountainside just a short time ago. Scott stood on both of his legs without a wobble. His broken bones had miraculously mended. He pulled off his own head bandage, which seemed to be bloody without reason, since there was no wound to be seen. We all joined in a prayer of thanksgiving to God for allowing Scott to lead us a while longer.

Eventually we crawled out of the canyon and onto the plain like bugs on a glass table, exposed to anyone who might be passing by, whether friend or foe. Yet we were surprisingly cheerful. Even the children were happy. It seemed as though the parents set the general mood for their children, as they do now. Anyone watching us might think that we had access to all the comforts of home, instead of a single change of clothing for each of us, and a shared cooking pot.

As the sound of bombs exploding in the distance reached our ears, we turned our heads as one. An agonized scream drifted across the distance, sending some children running for the safety of their mothers, hiding their faces in her clothes. Yet despite the sounds of battle, none of us questioned why God would send us out of the relatively safety of the mountains to the wide-open lands where we could be seen by any marauders. We trusted that we had been led here at the right time, for a specific purpose.

All trials make us better people. Going through tough times is like putting us through the refiner's fire, and makes us stronger. The more we go through hard times, the more faithful and caring we become. We cannot do anything without help from God. We must pray always and know that He will provide.

We set up our meager camp and got busy fixing an evening meal. When everyone had sufficient food, we offered up our nightly prayers and settled down to sleep.

I woke up while it was still night. I tried to go back to sleep, but it was no use. I was all through sleeping. I figured that I might as well get up and see if I could get something started for breakfast.

There were others up and moving around besides me, enough people that it seemed like something strange was going on. I looked toward the east where I expected the sky to be lightening in preparation for the coming day, but the horizon was the same darkness on the east as on the west. Scott pushed up his sleeve and peered at his watch face. "Why, it's nearly 8 a.m.," he said, his voice tinged with wonder.

What could it mean?

We said our morning prayers, then set about fixing food, making breakfast for the whole company. Once that was done, we watched the sky. Children asked their parents questions they had no answers for.

There was a lot of discussion over this day as dark as night, but no one seemed to know just what it meant. Some people wondered if this cover of darkness was for our benefit, to shield us from enemy eyes as we traveled. Others thought we should stay put and hope and pray that normal daylight would return.

We still hadn't reached any conclusion when we

fixed our mid-day meal. We watched our fires flickering bright orange in the darkness and wondered.

Several children napped in the afternoon. When they were awake, they didn't venture far from their mother's sides.

After dinner, we crawled into our blankets and sleeping bags, because there wasn't much else to do. It took awhile for me to get to sleep, staring upward and wondering at the strange event of darkness that lasted all day long.

Then a single voice in the darkness began telling scripture stories. It was a calm voice, soothing our company with tales of heroism, courage, and joy. I soon fell asleep with faith in my heart and an assurance that all would be well.

The next day was the same. We woke up to darkness, wondering why the daylight hours weren't light, but black as a starless night.

In spite of the darkness, I was able to make out the form of Walker as he made his way to the end of the grassy knoll we camped on, his face tipped up slightly as though scenting the air. He was quiet for a while, his back to us, listening to the sounds in the distance. I watched him, as did several others, more curious than afraid, for we had seen miracles and knew that when we exercised faith, God would be with us.

After a time, Walker turned and swept his eyes across our company. He smiled like an excited boy looking forward to fresh adventure. I turned and looked on the faces of my neighbors. What I saw made me stare in open-mouthed wonder. A faint white light glowed from within everyone I could see. My daughters, on the handcart next to mine, were radiating light, and looking so beautiful they nearly took my breath away. Everyone in our company was illuminated, almost like they had a soft spotlight on them, but I knew it came from within.

When I turned back to look at Walker, I saw that he was glowing, too. That was why I'd been able to see him moving around so well, but I just hadn't recognized it until now.

Suddenly my mind opened, and I knew that there were many groups like ours, waiting and watching for signs of the Savior's Second Coming. They waited patiently for their time to travel toward the New Jerusalem by whatever means they had. Cities of righteousness look forward to the Coming of the Lord with great anticipation and joy as they wait for the land to be cleansed from evil.

The wicked were destroying themselves, and when the time was right, all those who loved God and wished to live His law would be headed for the same place. I could see the people in the various cities, dressed in simple yet adequate clothing, laughing and dancing with joy, most without even a home to call their own, yet glowing with an inner light of Christ that they had earned for their righteousness and adherence to His teachings.

I saw a frenzy of activity as people in the cities made handcarts to use for their trek to New Jerusalem. Some people sorted through their provisions, ultimately leaving a lot of things behind for the final leg of their journey, even their tents. People sang while they worked, smiling and greeting one another in a friendly, loving manner.

Another bomb exploded in the distance.

"It's time to move down off this knoll," Walker said.

Scott moved toward Walker, his stride eating up big chunks of ground. He reached Walker's side and turned to face us. "He's right," Scott said. "In the morning, we move out."

I didn't know what to expect, but I knew we would be helped.

CHAPTER FOURTEEN
Traveling Companions

The next morning broke with a blush of light inching up the sky from below the eastern horizon. It seemed like so long since we'd seen the sun that it rose like a miracle over our encampment.

We loaded our carts, marveling with intense gratitude at the warmth and beauty of simple sunlight. I couldn't imagine ever taking the sunrise for granted again.

We set off down the bluff, reaching the flat prairie and making good time until people at the back of the company began calling out, "Look at that!"

"They're coming!"

"Oh, no!"

"They have tanks."

"There's an air patrol."

I turned and saw a sight that struck me with awe. A huge black flying machine shaped like a stealth bomber, but with rounded wing and a sleeker silhouette, must have been part helicopter, since it hovered over a body of men marching straight toward us with definite purpose. There was no question that they had seen us, and that we were their intended target. No cloak of invisibility surrounded us this time. My heart beat hard in my chest, my mouth went dry, and I shaded my eyes to get a better look at what was bearing down on us from the north.

Strangely enough, when I calmed down sufficiently to examine the feelings that coursed through my body, I discovered that they were more of excitement and eager anticipation than fear. I felt like a child on Christmas morning, facing a pile of gifts just for me.

Curious to know if my feelings were unique, I glanced on either side of me to see what others in my company were feeling. They watched the approaching army with smiles of welcome and relief. Without knowing exactly who they were, we knew in our hearts that we needn't fear them.

When the army drew closer, we could make out the individual soldiers, thousands of them sweeping down on us, all of them very tall. Some of them looked like they were at least seven feet tall. All of them had fair skin and a clear countenance. Their armor resembled armor worn in Bible times, but I later discovered that it was lightweight and impenetrable. The armor did nothing to conceal their broad shoulders and massive chests. They all looked as if they'd been working out with weights since the time they could crawl.

Members of the Lost Ten Tribes of Israel have returned. The reassurance came to my mind like a soft voice speaking words of comfort into my ear. *They will escort you to New Jerusalem.*

As the army from the Ten Tribes of Israel parted ranks to surround our company, I saw that not only were they accompanied by air support, but they also had weapons and tanks like I'd never seen before. Instead of the traditional tanks I was familiar with, these were close to the ground and seemed to glide over the terrain like a hovercraft, yet they had some kind of track that touched the earth beneath them. These tanks had an amazing suspension system that helped them move smoothly over the ground. The shape actually resembled a flying saucer, except that they were pointed at the front. They were about four times as wide as a normal tank, and about the same height. The guns on the tanks were massive.

Some of the soldiers converged on those of us who stood, clutching the drawbars of our handcarts, staring at their approach with open-mouthed wonder. As they drew closer, I saw that they were young men in their late teens or early twenties. Their faces wore smiles of welcome, and I couldn't help but smile back.

There were far more soldiers than handcarts. They surrounded our entire company with a circle of armored bodies, all of them facing east. I noticed a few more mature soldiers scattered among the ranks, taking on the role of leaders. This huge army seemed to know exactly what to do, as if they had been practicing this particular maneuver for years.

One of the soldiers approached me where I stood in front of my handcart. All I could do at first was stare up at him, speechless. He must have been about six and a half feet tall. Beneath his armor, he wore a long-sleeved shirt of a very strong fiber that I had never seen before. It molded around his bulging biceps and spanned his broad shoulders.

"I am Jeremiah," he said. "Allow me, please, to pull your handcart for you."

He moved his hand away from himself in a half circle, inviting me to step out of my place. Although he spoke English, his speech was tinged with an accent that reminded me of French, yet was softer than any French accent I'd ever heard. The deep voices resounding from the handcarts around me had the same mellow, soothing quality. There were no guttural sounds. Indeed, it almost sounded like they were singing as they spoke in their unique native tongue to one another, and that musical quality was still there when they spoke to us in English.

I dropped the drawbar of my handcart and moved out of the way. Jeremiah took my place, lifting the bar as effortlessly as if it had been a toothpick. As soon as all of us on handcart duty had traded places with a soldier, we moved out, surrounded by a human fortress and helped by amazingly strong men who seemed to be tireless.

In spite of their impressive physical size, the soldiers of the Ten Tribes were caring and gentle with us. I could feel kindness radiating from them. As far as human beings go, they were the best of the best.

When Christ spoke to his apostles in Jerusalem, he said, "And other sheep I have which are not of this fold: them also I must bring." (John 10:16). I believe that He was talking about other peoples, including the people of the Ten Tribes of Israel. I could sense their absolute love for the Lord.

We hadn't gone far when there was a disturbance to the south. I couldn't see beyond the wall of soldiers, but I heard shouting and the sound of many shots being fired.

Suddenly, the tank closest to me swiveled the barrel of its huge gun toward the noise, then spat out a long, straight burst of orange light, like a laser.

Instantly, the shooting outside of our formation stopped, and the soldiers on the south rim of our defenses regrouped and resumed their march.

I turned to stare at the tank that was gliding along as silently as if it ran on marshmallows.

"It shoots beams of pure energy," Jeremiah said, glancing down at me with a grin.

"How long does it take to reload?" I asked.

"There's no reloading. It uses the energy that's

around us all the time. It gathers it in and compresses it," he said in his soft accent.

"I'm so very glad you came along to help us."

"I've been planning for this all my life," Jeremiah said.

"How could you know you'd be doing this?" I asked, partly from curiosity, and partly because I loved to hear his accent when he spoke.

"We are from the tribe of Issachar," Jeremiah said. "All of us who are here received a calling when we were young boys, and have been taught and prepared since our youth, knowing that one day we would help the Tribes of Manasseh and Ephraim get to New Jerusalem." (Genesis 49:14-15)

"So you have to serve in this army?" I asked, thinking about the draft that registered young men for military service.

Jeremiah took me in with a gentle gaze. Yet underlying the softness, I could see a quality in his eyes that was as solid as steel. "I choose to do this," he said. "It is my calling, but it is also a privilege."

Several more times that day, the sounds of war approached us just before orange laser beams shot out of tanks or aircraft. With the Tribe of Issachar as our escort, nothing could stand in our way, not even enemy tanks. If anyone or anything from the opposing army fired on us, the huge guns of the Israelites would take it out. Most often it was the plane that did the shooting, as it had a better overview of what threat was coming our way. The opposing army coming against our escort was about as effective as ants swarming frantically out of an anthill, only to run into a hungry anteater.

"Why do they keep attacking?" I asked Jeremiah. "Don't they see they can't win?"

"They have eyes, but do not see," Jeremiah said. "We are strangers, so they want to fight us. They fear what they do not know, and fear is the opposite of all that our Father in Heaven is. They are so far gone in their depravity that they can only think of attacking, killing, destroying." He shook his head, his eyes full of sorrow. "Because of their aggression, their carnal desire for bloodshed is turned back onto their own heads, and they are the ones who end up being destroyed."

Jeremiah tipped his head up to glance toward Heaven, his eyes full of longing. "I can hardly wait for the Savior to come again and set this world on a peaceful course," he said.

I reached over and briefly touched his hand. "I love the Lord, too," I said. Then I glanced behind me at all the handcarts moving across the ground in a united group. "We all do."

It gave me great comfort to know that we had such great protection against those whose hearts and consciences were seared over to the point that the Holy Spirit couldn't even stir their lost souls to a remembrance of their God.

CHAPTER FIFTEEN

Gathering In The Flocks

The sun lowered in the sky and we stopped to make camp for the night. Jeremiah was conscientious and eager to help. He reminded me of my sons who had gone to fight with their father against the enemy, particularly Lance.

"Your mother sure taught you right," I said as I tugged on a crock of beans. The beans had been softening in water all day in preparation for the evening cooking pot.

Jeremiah reached over and pulled the crock up in his huge hands. "Yes, I have a good mother," he said.

Those in our company scurried about, fixing dinner for the army. I wished that we could have made something nicer than beans for these soldiers who were giving so much to see us safely to our destination, but we didn't have anything else. We gave them the best we had. After they ate, they thanked us most sincerely.

"It was delicious," Jeremiah said. Then he reached

into a pouch he had slung over his shoulder and pulled out some of his own food rations. "Here," he said, extending an unfamiliar looking block of something toward me. "You share with me, I share with you."

I accepted the tan-colored rectangle about the size of a granola bar. I turned it over in my hands. It looked like sugar cookie dough. Since I loved cookie dough, my mouth watered with anticipation. Yet if what I'd heard of standard army rations was any indication, what I held in my hand was likely to be less than tasty. Still, I wanted to show Jeremiah that I had good manners, too. He'd eaten the beans, I'd eat the bar. I hoped for the best and took a bite of the army food.

A smile of delight spread across my face. It was very good, even better than cookie dough. I ate the rest of it with relish, enjoying the sweet taste and the feeling of energy that pulsed through my body once I'd eaten the entire bar. It was surprisingly satisfying.

Over the course of the next two weeks, the Tribe of Issachar helped us travel twelve hours a day. Their food bars seemed to give us all the energy we needed to keep up with them. They fought our battles while we walked unmolested through the destruction that raged on all sides of us.

Occasionally, the ranks would open up and people like ourselves, carrying everything they had in this life, would join us. We greeted them warmly, delighted to have found more people who loved the Lord.

The newcomers told us that members of the opposing army would sometimes dress as wanderers, trying to catch any travelers unaware so they could heap their demented abuse upon them. There were some who had even approached the strange new armies that were scattered across the land, surrounding and defending travelers like ourselves. The disguised enemy claimed to seek protection, but the Ten Tribes of Israel had a gift of discernment that easily identified who was evil and who had a good heart, no matter whether they wore army fatigues or rags. Those who sought to deceive with feigned meekness were shot just as quickly as those who attacked our moving fortress with firing tanks.

Then, one memorable day, the ranks opened up to admit some newcomers into our circle of safety and I was amazed to see my sons, Kyle, Luke, Cody, and Lance step inside. Their eyes blinked in astonishment at the assembly of travelers who looked them over with smiles. My surprise quickly turned to delight, and I hurried toward my sons.

When they saw me, their eyes brightened. "Mom!" Kyle cried. When we met, I tried to hug them all at once, relishing the feel of their warm and living bodies, my sons, all grown up, yet still the children of my heart.

"Is it over?" I asked.

Kyle pulled back and dashed a hand against his eyes, still smiling. "It's not over, Mom. It won't be over until the enemy either converts to the Lord or is dead."

"Where's your father?" I asked.

Cody spoke up. "Dad went on ahead with a special company to scout out the place where we're going. We're almost there."

"How did you ever find us?" I asked.

"Word is out all over the place that there's this huge army that'll help you," Lance said.

"As long as you're good, that is," Kyle added.

"Yeah, it's like, 'stay away if you're a bad guy or you'll get split by an orange laser beam,'" Luke said. Then he shrugged. "I don't know exactly why we're here now, except that it feels like it's time to regroup or something."

I turned my head away from my sons and looked at the handcarts that seemed to stretch a mile ahead of us, and spread wide across the prairie. I noticed others greeting returned soldiers, too. One woman whose husband had left to fight the enemy long ago was now weeping with joy in his arms.

Then I looked behind us to see people and handcarts stretching as far back as I could see, at least another mile. We were certainly coming together, and the Army of Israel had us all covered.

Only those who know and love Christ will be helped through the battle, since the great army fights for righteousness and perceives what is in the hearts of men. Evil will not exist among us anymore.

CHAPTER SIXTEEN
Building New Jerusalem

On our last day of travel, a sense of energy ran through our company, a gentle current, yet sure as a breeze of fresh air. Everyone seemed to feel it. Jeremiah continued to pull my handcart as effortlessly as if it were a child's toy wagon, but his step was lighter and quicker.

Four hours into our day's travel, we halted. Normally we walked twelve hours, so I knew it wasn't time to set up evening camp. Soon the news passed through the ranks: we had arrived at the place where we would build New Jerusalem.

The flanks of protecting soldiers around us dissolved in a flurry of activity. The tanks and some of the foot soldiers moved out to the scarred hills on the perimeter of the chosen land and set up watch for any enemy soldiers.

The landscape was desolate, cleared and cleansed in preparation for building a city for the followers of Christ.

Old Jerusalem is also a gathering place for the righteous. Since we were on a different continent, it was up to us to build New Jerusalem.

As I set up camp for our first night there, I was startled by a familiar voice calling my name. I turned to see James hurrying toward me, his smile as bright and welcome as the sun after those two days of darkness we experienced on the bluff.

"James!" I cried, heading for his arms. My family was reunited at last, and my joy was full.

Our company soon organized into work details. Each of our talents was taken into consideration, much like in the tent cities, where those who like to cook are in charge of meals, those who like to teach are the teachers, and those who like to build are the ones who make plans for erecting houses and churches, temples and synagogues.

The city organizers got busy laying out plots and streets for the city. Although many buildings that remained in the area were either bombed or vandalized, we discovered a brick plant that survived the ravages of war. As we explored further, we realized that amidst the destruction, the Lord had preserved many things that were useful in helping to build up New Jerusalem.

The people from the Ten Tribes had far greater capabilities than we did. Their vast knowledge was astounding. They headed up the planning and building projects, using technology that far surpassed what we have today. With all their abilities, and their faith in God, it was no wonder that He was able to hide them from the rest of the world until He saw fit to bring them forth in His own good time.

We moved ahead with our city building at a pace that was previously unknown to man on earth. In less than a month, we were moving into our new houses. Everyone chose the way they wanted their house built, and it was great fun knowing we could have any kind of house we liked. People with more children naturally chose a bigger home, but no one was interested in building a huge house just for show. No one was greedy or pretentious. Some people had gazebos, if they enjoyed spending time sitting out of doors. Some had porches, some chose to add on a balcony or bay window, some surrounded their homes with wide expanses of grass where they could run and play and keep pets. Others had almost no yard at all, because they didn't like doing yard work. Some chose to live in apartment buildings. There were those who liked to work with animals, and they were assigned larger tracts of land to grow animal feed and to house livestock.

I was very comfortable in our new home, grateful to again have a solid roof and walls, running water and an indoor toilet. With the Ten Tribes' knowledge of technology, everyone was more comfortable than we'd ever been. The concrete they made could last for centuries. With everyone's help, including the children, New Jerusalem quickly took shape, yet was ever expanding as more people arrived.

The centerpiece of the city was a wonderful temple complex of elegant buildings topped with white spires, surrounded by beautiful gardens filled with sculptures. Wide pathways led to each of the buildings, and the entire area carried a deep feeling of peace. We regularly gathered there to worship the Lord.

The families of the Ten Tribes of Israel also came to live with us. The women and children wore simple dresses of heavy woven cloth. Since I love to sew, I made sure to examine the fabric. It was nothing I was familiar with. It was very durable and stain resistant. The clothing design was simple, just a single front and back piece sewn together. They usually wore a sash around their waist. The boys wore pants and a contrasting shirt of simple design.

I was delighted to meet Jeremiah's mother, a beautiful woman with stately carriage and kind gray eyes. When I hugged her, I felt enveloped with love.

"Your son Jeremiah was so kind to us," I said.

"I'm glad to hear it," she answered.

"Now that I've met you, I can easily see why Jeremiah turned out to be such a fine young man."

His mother smiled. "Your sons are fine men, too," she said, her musical accent as sweet to my ears as her kind words.

As we all assembled and lived among each other,

it was interesting to note that the religion anyone in our city came from did not matter at all. We are all children of God, and being His children is our common denominator. Many different faiths have a lot of truth. Over the centuries, there have been several debates, some rather violent, over which church is true. The very act of arguing and fighting and warring over religion is in direct opposition to Christ's teachings. He asks us to love one another, to treat each other with kindness, whether we are scholars of scriptures or just learning how to pray.

There may be more truth in some churches than others, but you have to understand that some people are not ready for the more advanced teachings. Living the Ten Commandments is hard for a lot of people, so they need simpler laws. As long as they desire to draw closer to Christ, then their hearts are in the right place. As long as they're making progress, that is the main criteria, and they can work through the steps at their own pace.

There was no discrimination in New Jerusalem, only love in everyone's hearts. There was no selfishness. There was no self-aggrandizement or boasting. Our daily conversations were made up of words of kindness, humor and encouragement.

New people arrived almost daily. If any of them came in with a chip on their shoulder or grudges against another, they either learned to let go of it, or else they chose to move on, because they weren't comfortable being among us.

From time to time, other companies of travelers arrived, guarded by soldiers of the Ten Tribes. We welcomed them into the growing city with great joy.

With these ever-increasing numbers, we found the need to form a human resources committee, made up of those who enjoyed meeting and interacting with people. Their only job was to direct newcomers where to go in the city, and to help them get settled. They were in constant demand.

Ultimately, New Jerusalem grew to cover hundreds of square miles. Gardens grew vegetables to huge proportions, food full to nearly bursting with vitamins and nutrition. We ate meat sparingly. The bulk of our protein came from chickens and eggs. No one had more than they needed. We were all healthy and vibrant, looking forward with eager anticipation to the arrival of our Savior.

We lived in continual peace, protected against those who sought to harm us by the army on the city perimeter. We were taught greater truths by prophets of God, as well as angels who visited us from time to time. They taught us the higher law of consecration that we had to learn to live before Christ could come to us. No one was forced to learn anything new, but either they chose to live the law, or they would not see Christ. Yet everyone I knew wanted to learn as much as they could to prepare for Christ's coming.

Everybody within the city's borders had spiritual gifts. We worked and studied with hearts full of joy, knowing that Christ's coming was ever nearer. We wanted to have everything perfect for Christ when he arrived, so we worked together to build a city worthy of Him to enter.

Some of the newcomers said they came to the city because rumors of a prospering city with industrious, cheerful people were spreading rapidly.

"It's said that you must not go there unless you love the Lord," one of them told me. "If you try to get in and you are a faker or pretender, you will not make it. You will die. Either you will be shot, or you will turn into a pillar of salt or something."

My eyes widened. "Has that really happened?"

The newcomer shrugged. "I only know that most of the wicked are afraid to get too close. Several of their number have launched an attack on New Jerusalem and have never returned. Some think that if they even so much as look on this city, they'll turn to dust or be smitten."

It was interesting to see that some of those who came into our midst actually wore the dreaded green and brown camouflage suits of the invading army. Yet those who protected our borders used their sense of discernment to tell if the enemy soldiers had turned their hearts around. Those who made it in were the ones who could not abide the cruel practices of their fellow soldiers. They were the ones who had put a stop to wanton torture or senseless killings whenever it was in their power to do so. No matter what their background, all who wanted peace and safety were welcomed to New Jerusalem.

Our former enemies told of their leader's surprise at the resistance they encountered in America. "In other countries, the citizens submitted to us, like deer who run from danger. When they are pursued and caught, they give up the fight," one said. "At first we thought Americans were the same. We took some towns by surprise and the people submitted. But we didn't know that many of them were actually as fierce as bears, and we only saw them hibernating. Eventually they roused, and fought fiercely to the death."

"Especially in the country," another former soldier said. "More of the people outside of the city had guns and rifles, and knew how to use them."

A different soldier added, "The cities where people had no weapons were easy to conquer. We just went in and pointed our guns at them and the people did what we told them to. But as we moved into the country, word of our coming spread. There were many places where almost all the homes were empty, because people saw us coming or heard that we were on the way and ran from us, giving a warning everyplace they passed through."

I thought of Kurt, and the message he had brought to us. I hoped that he had found peace.

"Not all of our leaders were organized," another soldier added. "Coming together from different countries as we did, there was often a difference of opinion. Some of our leaders never listened to their counterparts, and some encouraged acts of brutality. They left our wounded behind, so we lost faith in them. I admired the courage and bravery of all of you who lived here and worked to defend your land. I sensed a power that was with you, one that was greater than the power of our weapons, our soldiers, and even our commanders. It touched something within me, here." He put his open palm over his chest. "That is why I decided I'd rather join you than fight against you."

Another man who'd been living among us for some time spoke up. "I was one of the invading army left behind, with a bullet in my leg and one in my chest," he said. "When I was utterly helpless, some citizens found me and bandaged my wounds. I could not believe it. I was still in my uniform, so they knew who I was. They fed me and cared for me until I was well again. I realized I had no allegiance to the invaders. They are heartless men who care nothing for anyone but themselves. I now fight for a higher power. I am on God's side."

Many of those who found their way to New Jerusalem said that they were led and helped by fearless men who were unfailingly kind.

Their stories were similar to Greg's unlikely experience of meeting three men in the mountains when the very lives of his children depended on finding shelter. Often, when the recipients of the acts of kindness would turn to thank their benefactors, there would be no one there. They had been helped by messengers of God.

Many cultures have been preparing for these events. Native American Indians have had visions of the Last Days for centuries. People in South America are converting to Christianity in droves, becoming the fastest culture to accept Christ.

Native Americans are traditionally a culture of storytellers. There is a certain tribe of Indians living high in the mountains of South America. They are not a physically imposing people; the men do not generally stand much taller than five feet. The women usually stop growing at just over four feet tall. The first born of a family, whether boy or girl, is the designated storyteller. They are taught the family's history from the time of Moses. Every child, no matter their birth order, is taught of the creation of earth, and their original parents, Adam and Eve.

Every child knows that they come from greatness, that they are children of God, and that they are precious in His eyes. After they are taught their origins and learn that they are people of worth, then they are taught about what their purpose is on earth, and where they are going.

Visions, dreams, and near death experiences are a way of life with this people. They expect them. It's not like other cultures, where people who may experience these things keep them to themselves. These people teach that Christ should be openly sought. They are very spiritual people who've been watching the signs and waiting for Him to come. They do all the things they've been told to do. They already know about the Lord's Second Coming, they knew it generations before we did. They made a mistake once, thinking Cortez was the one. The miracle is, that even after they realized they had the wrong man, they didn't give up faith. They kept on believing and watching for the right one.

When these choice Indian people finally arrived in New Jerusalem, they added many wonderful teachings to what we already knew. Although Spanish was not their native language, they understood it, so we were able to communicate with them. We also relied on the gift of tongues. They were a delightful people, and very happy to be among us.

After we'd been established in our city for a few years, the warring sounds in the distance ceased. The border patrols came home. We were comfortable and busy in our huge city.

Then a group of people arrived who were so beautiful, I could hardly take my eyes off them. They glowed, radiating a goodness that surpassed even that of the Ten Tribes of Israel. I felt drawn to them, wanting to be near enough to bask in their peaceful presence. Whenever any one of them looked at me, I felt engulfed with pure love.

Members of the Ten Tribes rushed forward to greet the newcomers as if they were long-lost friends. "Enoch and his people have returned," Jeremiah said, looking on the joyous reunion with a broad smile on his face.

I was astounded. "Returned? Where?" I asked.

"Enoch was taken to Heaven without tasting of death," Jeremiah said. (Hebrews 11:5) "He and his followers have now returned. This means that Christ will arrive to live among us any day."

My heart swelled with complete joy, so full that it filled my chest, rose in my throat, then filled my head, forcing tears of pure happiness from my eyes. It was as if my spirit soared to the Heavens in delight at the mere thought of having Christ come to live in our midst. I fell to my knees and bowed my head in deep gratitude.

CHAPTER SEVENTEEN
At Christ's Side

A large hand descended onto my shoulder, its strength equal to its gentleness. I was instantly flooded with warmth and loving reassurance. I wiped my eyes with the back of my hand and raised my head, focusing on the face of Jesus Christ above me, His blue eyes filled with compassion.

I got up from my knees and blinked a couple of times, adjusting myself to being back in the pure white room. The screen was once again a cold white expanse. Yet what I had seen was so real, I felt as though I'd lived every event that was shown to me through the Window of Life.

I turned to Christ, my eyes brimming with fresh tears. He drew me into a loving embrace, and then told me more of the things He wanted everyone to know.

There is no such thing as Doomsday, even though we've been taught from the very beginning of time that there is an end to all things on earth. The end of our current earthly era is the beginning of a new time of great peace and joy. Father in Heaven wants all of us to return safely to Him, but we will only be happy in His presence if we've earned it. We must know within ourselves that we deserve to be with God in the end, not that He was nice to let us in. We wouldn't be happy or comfortable there if we didn't truly do our part. The only Doomsday we might experience is one of our own making, a Doomsday that we will feel within ourselves if we don't live up to our potential, but it will be no one else's.

We cannot go on thinking that nothing will ever happen to us, but we need to remember that we are saved through Christ and only through Christ. Fear is the killer. The devil loves to bring fear. If there is fear, there is no faith. Faith is the key, knowing that Christ is with us always, and will help us get through tough times in His own omnipotent way. We cannot always understand why things are the way they are, but if we truly know that He loves us completely, we can trust Him to help us through anything, in His own perfect timetable.

If there is nothing else gained from this book other than the knowledge that we must have a relationship with the Lord, then my job is done.

How do you get a relationship with the Lord? Pray, pray, pray. Weary the Lord as many times a day as you can. Ask him to be with you, to teach you. There will be answers in the scriptures for you. So search, ponder, and pray.

Another important key is to start right now to diligently strive to hear the promptings of the holy Spirit. It may not be a prompting to do very much, but go forward with it anyway. Get to know the feelings that come into your heart. It might be like a small voice or a feeling. Do not excuse it, saying it's just your own idea. Answer it. It may be something simple, like call a friend. If prompted, do it!

Learning to listen to the small voice is like a child learning a new word. It takes practice for him to understand what he hears. First, he understands what is said, then he learns to speak. It's the same with learning to follow the promptings of the Spirit. One has to feel what is heard first, then one can act upon the feeling.

You need to decide now if you are going to be willing to follow the promptings of the Holy Spirit. It's like teaching our children to decide now whether or not they will take illegal drugs if they have the chance. Make the choice before the crisis happens. Decide now if you're willing to leave all the comforts of your home. Are we willing to leave our comfortable beds, our modern stoves, our heated showers? We must choose to follow the Lord. A last-second choice may not be the right one if we haven't practiced listening and following the promptings of the Spirit. Whatever happens, do not let fear take over or you could make the wrong choice.

As soon as you get used to hearing and feeling the Spirit, the rest will fall into place. As time goes by, you may hear words come into your head in a voice that is not yours. This can be a step toward having a personal relationship with Christ. Get to know His voice so well that there is no question that it is His.

With the Lord by your side, nothing is scary. He can be your best friend. He is someone who loves you perfectly, absolutely, just as you are right now. He offers no judgment, no matter what you've done or not done. All He has in His heart for you is pure love, so boundless that He died for you.

Do not expect anything, as you are not entitled to anything. Instead, cultivate an attitude of always feeling grateful, even for the smallest things in your life.

Know that the Last Days will be great and wonderful for the pure in heart. This is when the Lord comes to live with us! What a glorious situation to be in!

CHAPTER EIGHTEEN
Return to Mortality

After my experience with the Window of Life, Christ took me out of the room to see a few other places, but I knew that my time in this beautiful sphere was drawing to an end.

I sometimes wonder, if Christ hadn't made the promise to take me back when we met in the surgery room of the hospital, whether I would have chosen to return or not. The sense of peace in the post-life realm was incredible. The sense of being loved permeates your whole being. You are surrounded with love, you feel it, you breathe it, you taste it. As much as you may be loved in your homes and families on earth, it just can't compare to what is felt in the life after this one.

But my decision wasn't up for review. Christ keeps His promises. And I had made a promise to myself. I knew, deep inside, that my children still needed me.

Leaving that beautiful place was the hardest thing I have ever had to do, or will ever have to do in my life.

Christ took my hand and led me back to the operating room. I cried as I looked down on my bloated body. It was absolutely still, and looked like a stranger.

Someone in the room called out, "She's not breathing."

Time on earth is not the same as it is in Heaven. To the people in the operating room, I had only been dead for a few moments, while it seemed to me that I had been gone much longer.

A flurry of activity erupted, a machine was wheeled into the room, and someone took hold of a couple of flat paddles like I'd seen in TV shows, the kind they put on a patient's chest, call "Clear!" and then shock the patient's body to the point that it jumps and arches, as though in pain. It was not a pleasant prospect.

Christ took hold of my chin in His gentle fingers and turned my face toward him. As tears continued to well up in my eyes and spill down my cheeks, I saw that Christ was crying, too.

"Never forget that I love you," He said.

My heart melted. It was so hard to leave Him.

"Remember that I will always be with you," He said. The compassion in His voice resonated in my soul as he bent forward and kissed my cheek.

"Share what you have learned," Christ said. "Help bring my sheep back to me."

I embraced the Savior, and told Him that I would do as He asked, because I love Him with all my heart.

The next instant, I was back in my body. With one gasp, I drew in the breath of life. In that split second, I was hit with all the pain of my hemorrhaging body. I ached, I burned, I cried out, I wanted to be dead.

At last, they gave me anesthesia, but I didn't go back to the place of peace I'd just come from. I went into a black unconsciousness.

When I woke up, the surgery was done.

I was alive, but I was despondent. My baby, although it couldn't have survived, had been taken away from me, and I hurt all over, both spiritually and physically. I didn't have any memories of my heavenly experience to comfort me, either. That all came to me later, and when it did, I welcomed the flood of those infinitely sweet memories of peace, love, and joy.

Now as I go through each day, I plan on living better and loving everyone I see. It's my hope and prayer that with the help of the information in this book, we can all have a chance to be there when Christ comes again.

About the Authors

Suzanne Freeman lives in a small town with her husband James and their ten children. She loves to cook and sew, and she uses these talents to bless the lives of those around her.

You can contact Suzanne through her publisher, at **public_relations@springcreekbooks.com** to arrange speaking opportunities about her experiences.

Shirley Bahlmann is the co-author of Suzanne's previous book *Led by the Hand of Christ*. She has also written several volumes of true pioneer stories, *Against All Odds, Isn't That Odd, Even Love Is Odd,* and *Unseen Odds*. Shirley also has published novels entitled *Walker's Gold* and *Fool's Gold,* with the sequel *Bands of Gold* in the works.

She is the wife of award-winning sports writer Bob Bahlmann and they are the parents of six sons. Please visit her website at **www.shirleybahlmann.com** to see her writing tips and learn more about her upcoming books.

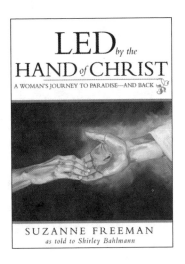